WHAT WILL OUTLAST ME?

Essays

Sarah K. Lenz

WHAT WILL OUTLAST ME?
Copyright © 2023 Sarah K. Lenz
All Rights Reserved.
Published by Unsolicited Press.
Printed in the United States of America.
First Edition.

No part of this book may be used or reproduced in any manner whatsoever without written permission except in the case of brief quotations embodied in critical articles or reviews.

Attention schools and businesses: for discounted copies on bulk orders, please contact the publisher directly. Booksellers can order copies from Ingram.

For information contact:
Unsolicited Press
Portland, Oregon
www.unsolicitedpress.com
orders@unsolicitedpress.com
619-354-8005

Front Cover Design: Kathryn Gerhardt
Editor: Robin LeeAnn

ISBN: 978-1-956692-53-2

For
S.L.

Author's Note

I have strived to be as accurate as possible in my recall of events, but memory is a slippery thing. The very act of retrieving a memory alters it. Employing a memory to serve a story, as I've done countless times in these pages, reshapes the initial impression, and possibly distorts it. Those that have experienced these events alongside me may remember what happened differently. I have constructed dialogue from memory, and where possible, have relied on my journals and photo albums to corroborate details. Some names have been changed to protect privacy or to avoid confusing duplicate names.

TABLE OF CONTENTS

DRIVING THE SECTION LINE	11
SLIBNY'S FIRE	29
LIGHTNING FLOWERS	42
SHOOTING ON IZARD STREET	58
KILLING CHICKENS	71
MAKING HEADCHEESE	85
A BOOK FROM MY GRANDMA, A MESSAGE FROM THE GRAVE	98
HOLY DIMINISHMENT	111
A CASE FOR RUBBERNECKING	127
THE BELLY OF DESIRE	141
SO MANY WAYS	157
WHAT CANNOT BE HELPED	173
PANCAKES ARE JUST PANCAKES	185
CANCER IS CLICHÉ	194
FROM BIRTH TO BONE	208
BEFORE IT'S NIGHT ONCE MORE	219

WHAT WILL OUTLAST ME?

Essays

DRIVING THE SECTION LINE

"When I die, I want you to dump my ashes on Henry's Hill," Dad said. We sat at his kitchen table in his trailer house on lot #1, Del Mar Mobile Home Court, in Doniphan, Nebraska, where he now lived alone.

"Okay," I said. "Why are you telling me this?"

"Someone needs to know." He had a USA Gold cigarette—the brand he switched to when Marlboros got too expensive—pinched between his leathery fingers. His other hand clasped a can of Old Milwaukee red label. On the table a scrape the size of a dinner plate marked the spot where, decade after decade, he had rested his beer. Like a cataract or a contusion, the Formica's wood print had been scraped down by the bottom of the can.

"Now, I mean it. You're to cremate me and dump my ashes on Henry's Hill."

He had reached the familiar state of drunkenness in which he repeats himself, forgetting moments ago what he just said. He would reiterate this thread of conversation over and over, until he ran out of beer or stumbled off to bed to pass out. I took a sip of my beer. It was late May, and I was back from grad school in Georgia for a visit. I only saw Dad once or twice a year, and as much as it was tedious to sit there in the same

WHAT WILL OUTLAST ME?

conversation loop, something in me felt duty bound. My husband, Kent, had stayed behind in Georgia. I'd called him earlier that afternoon because I needed to tell someone about how depressing it was to see how my dad's life had diminished. Kent reminded me: "You're the best thing he's done. He's proud of you and loves you. You can handle this visit." Though I appreciated his words, filial obligation weighed heavy. I thought about my younger sister who hadn't spoken to our father in over a decade, not since he showed up to her wedding drunk. Part of me envied her for the clean break she'd made.

"The kitchen looks nice," I offered, trying to get him out of the conversational rut. Since my last visit, he'd remodeled, put in new oak cabinets and shiny laminate floors.

"It was a bitch putting that sink in," Dad said, waving his beer can toward the new stainless-steel fixture. "I broke two sets of brackets, had to make three trips to Menards. Looks pretty good, though. Sandy picked it all out before she got sick." He paused, took another long swig of beer. "Dump my ashes on Henry's Hill. You got that?"

"Yes, you already told me." I wished Sandy were here. She'd been Dad's girlfriend. The last time I saw her we sat at this same table drinking Diet Dr. Pepper (her favorite). She told me: "Your father doesn't have a malicious bone in his body. Sure, he drinks, but he wouldn't hurt a flea." She lived with him until she got sick last winter. A kidney infection had turned into sepsis, and she'd spent three weeks in the ICU. When I was visiting for Christmas last year, Dad had taken me to see her in the hospital. Because of the excruciating pain she was in, the doctors put her in a medically induced coma. I thought back to how heartbroken I had been for my dad that day.

"Sandy, it's me, Rolland. Sarah's here too," he said as he leaned over her hospital bed. He gently brushed her mussed hair from her forehead and gave her a kiss. Her eyes fluttered open for a moment, but I'm sure they couldn't register what they saw. His eyes filled with tears. When he saw me watching him, I looked away, focusing on the coloring book pages hanging listlessly around the room, which Sandy's grandkids had brought.

When we left the hospital, it was brutally cold. The wind blew full tilt from the north, rattling the flagpole's rope and pulley. In the car, Dad tamped a cigarette from his pack and lit it. My breath streamed out in cloudy wisps, mingling with his cigarette smoke.

He finally spoke, "It sure is hard to see her like that, isn't it?"

I nodded. Afraid that he was going to cry again, I stared at the empty parking space next to us where someone had dropped a banana peel. Splayed flat across the frozen asphalt, its blackened edges curled in on itself in frozen helplessness.

"Hey, get me another beer, will ya?"

I got up from the table. Though there was a whole case of Old Milwaukee in his fridge, there was little food. A crumpled McDonald's bag with half a burger inside sat on one shelf, a dozen eggs and a package of hotdogs on the another.

"Do you miss Sandy's cooking?" I asked as I handed him a beer.

WHAT WILL OUTLAST ME?

"Everyday." He belched, then cracked the new beer open and slid the tab sideways, a gesture I have seen him repeat hundreds, if not thousands of times.

The next day, Dad and I went on what he called his "nostalgia tour." We headed north for 60 miles, driving his twenty-year-old Geo Prizm, and ended up in Geranium Township at the top of Henry's Hill. Supposedly it was the highest point in Valley County. We stood at its summit, just before the elevation dropped off into a ravine. A rotten fence post covered with lichen jutted from the earth, trailing a curl of rusted barbed wire. A few orange cedar trees and smaller clumps of spiked yucca dotted the pasture. From that vantage we saw what used to be our homeplace, 160 acres of farmland that—until my father lost it—had been in the Krahulik family for five generations, since 1903.

The two-story farmhouse, red barn, and grain bins occupied a quarter-mile section. We took in the expanse of cornfields and feedlots full of cattle, all the land that used to be his. It was a geographical center. Point your finger at the middle of Nebraska on a map; you'll land on it. It was my father's center, too. As if by gravity or some other invisible force, he was pulled there now, even decades later. I imagined shaking his ashes from an urn, and how they would scatter on the wind and land on the soil he used to plow.

"Here's the spot."

"Is it legal?" I asked Dad, wondering about who owned the land, about trespassing laws and burial laws.

"Better to ask forgiveness than permission."

He flicked his cigarette down off the embankment, giving me something else to worry about. The combination of dry wind and parched grass was perfect for brush fires. The wind made a high-pitched groaning as it swept over the cottonwoods and made me feel spooked. It had a sinister quality, unlike any place I had ever lived, not like the soupy humid air of the Deep South, nor the arid air of Idaho's foothills. Those places didn't have real wind, unlike here where the weather was mercurial.

"When'd you start farming?" I asked.

"Let's see, that would have been spring of '77." He squinted into the distance between the pasture and cornfields. He didn't see well anymore and needed cataract surgery. "Get me those binoculars in the glove box, will ya?"

He had parked the white Geo a few feet away in the empty hay field. I got the binoculars for him.

"I should have known I'd have bad luck," he continued, binoculars held tight against his eyes as he focused in on the homeplace. "That first year, corn got hailed out. Lost everything." Then he paused, set the binoculars down. "That kind of thing makes it hard not to be superstitious. Makes you wonder about God."

Those words hadn't sunk in before he changed the subject: "This used to be a Pawnee Indian lookout." This was just speculation on his part, another kind of faith, the only kind he can muster anymore.

After Henry's Hill, Dad drove the section lines, roads that follow both the compass coordinates and the mile-by-mile Jeffersonian patchwork. We drove past a pasture where I used to tag along during calving season. Once I'd watched from the

WHAT WILL OUTLAST ME?

pickup as Dad helped a Black Angus birth a white-faced calf. We drove past a freshly planted cornfield, a giant swath of brown corduroy. Its loam perfumed the air. We drove past another field Dad used to farm, where in the summer we checked the irrigation pivots. The sky spread so deep blue it hurt my eyes. It hit me how I used to feel a sense of peace on those summer nights. As dusk settled in, so did the feeling that all was right in the world. Driving through fields of corn as tall as the pickup truck, we had seen green leaves gleaming with moisture, the arching spray from the pivot hitting the last rays of sunlight, haloing the world in fleeting rainbows. I understood the ache of Dad's loss.

We passed by grain bins with the Chief Industries logo—an Indigenous person in profile wearing a white and red feathered headdress, depicted in blockish rectangles. Dad retired from Chief a few years ago, but he still wore the same factory work clothes: navy blue Dickies workpants held on his bony frame by thick, red suspenders. He had worked in fabrication and welding. I thought about the downward trajectory of his life, how he went from producing the grain that went into the bins to building the bins in a factory.

The Geo crawled slowly along the gravel roads soft at the edges from a recent rain. The windows were down. Waylon Jennings played on the tape deck. Dad barely said a word as we drove. I wondered what he was thinking about. All his talk about his funeral plans made me feel pity. What does it feel like to look back at your life and have little to show for it but a string of failures?

Dad had returned to the homeplace in the late '70s to run the cattle-and-corn operation with his father and brother during the Earl Butz era of American agriculture, the beginning of rapid consolidations and the "get big or get out" mentality. The Krahuliks wanted to get big, and it seemed like the perfect time: grain prices soared because of a Russian grain shortage. Dad had just suffered his first divorce and been discharged from the Air Force. With few other prospects, farming was his fallback, but he quickly fell in love with it. He also fell in love with my mother that summer. They eloped in September. Four years later I was born.

We passed another farmstead, a two-story farmhouse surrounded by cattle feedlots.

"There's Treptow's. You remember them?"

"Sure." Dad said so little that I wasn't sure if I was supposed to elaborate on my response or match his few words. I remembered Calvin Treptow had tried to help Dad save the farm in the 1980s when things started to fall apart. At the height of his prosperity, Dad—along with my grandpa and uncle—farmed 2,400 acres, hayed 1,000 acres, and fed 800 head of cattle. They'd managed to expand by taking out hundreds of thousands of dollars in loans for more land, more machinery, and more glistening black cattle. The bankers handed out loans like candy because the land was always there as collateral. Then the bubble burst. The bank that held the loans went under. Immediate repayment was due. Grandpa Harvey sold all his machinery and cattle and still fell short. The 160-acre homeplace—to which Grandpa held the deed—went to the FDIC, which foreclosed on the land and the farmhouse. Dad

WHAT WILL OUTLAST ME?

asked Calvin Treptow for help. Somehow, Dad convinced Calvin to buy the homeplace and rent it back to him: a farmer's agreement, sealed with a handshake.

It didn't work out. After eight years, Calvin put the homeplace up for sale. Hoping he had just enough collateral to swing it, my dad applied for a loan. During the three days' wait for loan approval, the farm sold to someone else. I wondered if he drank because he lost the farm or if he lost the farm because he drank. It was an impossible, tumbling riddle.

I had been in second grade when we moved to a house in the small town of Ord, county seat of Valley County. All of Dad's farm equipment—planters, cultivators, combines—were auctioned to pay the bank. Dad took a job as an itinerant construction worker, welding girders and pouring concrete to build bridges and freeway ramps. In ever-widening circles, he followed the work away from his geographic center.

We drove on. Dad wanted to take me to the one-room school where my grandma had taught and where he and my uncles went to school until the 8th grade before transferring to Ord High School. At first, he couldn't find the schoolhouse. I worried about his mind. Surely forty years of alcoholism shoots memory to hell. Apparently, a farmer moved the schoolhouse building—on the back of a haystack mover—so now it sat in someone's back pasture. For forty-five minutes we drove up and down the section lines before he turned off the road and nosed the car up to a three-strand barbed-wire gate.

"Get the gate, will ya?"

Now I was less worried about trespassing and more worried about cattle. What if there was a bull? Reluctantly, I unbuckled the seatbelt that Dad teased me for wearing. Maybe he had a point. We hadn't met another car all day, nor exceeded forty-five miles per hour. Still, I knew how loose gravel could fishtail a car without warning.

The gate was jerry-rigged with baling wire and pliers. I laid the fence down flat, so the wire could be driven over. I refastened the gate and got back in the car. Dad found a cow-path rut in the pasture and followed it along the hills. At ten miles per hour, the car pitched like a boat over swells.

Behind a cluster of cedars, I saw it: a sagging schoolhouse, its clapboards weathered to a dull gray. Dad got out of the car, stubbed his cigarette in the grass, and rattled out a spittle-laden cough. He opened the front door and walked in like he owned the place. The building's graceful decay made it more beautiful than it ever could have been in its prime. Peeking through rot holes in the roof, sunlight dappled the warped floorboards and flashed across a broken wall. Plaster crumbled off wood lathes like frosting off a cake. Long skins of milk green paint peeled from the remaining plaster.

Dad wandered around the ruined school room.

"Look, here's the old belltower," he said. I looked up. The belfry was empty. "Remember that old bell we had on the farm? Here's where it came from. Your grandma got it when they closed the school. But it sold at the foreclosure auction. Remember?"

I did, and I understood why he called this his "nostalgia tour." Each landmark or object was a way for him to tell me—without so many words—the stories I already knew. If I were

WHAT WILL OUTLAST ME?

his legacy, he needed to be reassured that I knew his stories and that they would live on after he's gone.

When I was growing up, Mom had used the school bell for a dinner gong. My favorite chore was ringing it when supper was ready. No matter how far away Dad worked on the homeplace, the bell summoned him. Only a sound that crisp and loud could pierce the windy, almost treeless land. It travelled farther than my loudest screams (meant to provoke the tom turkeys into gobbling), louder than the howl of Spike, our border collie, and louder than the cries of wild coyotes. It filled the space with its resounding, mellifluous tolling. I felt it in my throat and lungs, almost tasted it as it caught and scattered in the wind. In this small family ritual, maybe we had wished the gong could put demons to flight and protect us from hail and tornadoes.

*

After a few minutes, I felt anxious in the schoolhouse's silence, broken only by the wind swishing ominously through the cedars. A mud-caked four-wheeler parked in the backroom reminded me that we were trespassing again. Did the owner carry a gun? Might he think we were there to steal his property? Dad wasn't worried. If needed, he could explain why we were there.

Three miles later, Dad pulled up to a row of ancient Osage orange trees a mile south of the homeplace. His weathered face matched the gnarled trees' wrinkled bark. He pointed to a field of corn seedlings.

"There used to be a road here," he said. "I walked this road to school and back, straight across the section line." I tried to imagine my father as a child but soon abandoned the idea. Instead I thought about how things fade and disappear. Grandma Krahulik used to pick the lumpy, green Osage oranges. She put them in the bottom of her china cabinets and closets to repel bugs, but it seemed to me that like the school bell, they protected us from other things, too. Perhaps the Osages warded off the evil spirits carried by those dry prairie winds. I wished they were in season so I could have taken some home with me. But even if they had been, I wouldn't have been able to get them through airport security. No one knows what they're used for anymore.

We drove past yet another cornfield, and this one was planted in Cargill seeds. The test plot signs were already set into the ground at each row, the seed hybrid number printed below the yellow and black Cargill logo, a sideways seed that looked like a teardrop.

"Hey, that's my old brand," Dad said. I remembered that too, but it wasn't a pleasant memory. Because Dad planted Cargill-brand seed, his seed distributor gave him Cargill swag: trucker hats and jackets, even a yardstick.

It was the winter of 1987, and I was a kindergartener. My mother was pregnant with my little sister. Mom had turned my old bedroom on the first floor into the nursery, and my bedroom was relocated upstairs to the bedroom that had been my father's when he was a boy. The room frightened me. Most nights when I couldn't sleep, I'd sneak downstairs to the living room where Dad drank beer and watched M*A*S*H reruns. He let me snuggle in his lap, breathing in his scent of

WHAT WILL OUTLAST ME?

tobacco and beer: earthy and malty, both sour and sweet, until I fell asleep. After a while, anytime I woke up alone in the room, I ran downstairs and refused to go back to bed unless Mom or Dad laid next to me until I fell asleep.

One night when I tried to sneak downstairs, Dad ambushed me. He sat on the landing, a can of beer in one hand, and his Cargill yardstick in the other. The yardstick was several inches wide, a quarter inch thick, and painted bright-yellow and stamped with that teardrop-shaped logo. When he saw me, he cracked the yardstick—hard—on the linoleum. I burst into tears.

He jabbed the yardstick at my bare legs, then tipped his head back, swigging the dregs from his can and threw it down the stairs. The can clattered as it bounced down the steps and rolled toward my mother, who was sitting at the kitchen table, too terrified to stop him. I cried gasping, hysterical tears, losing my breath as I tried to escape the dark terror of the room, only to be goaded back into it by the jabs of the yardstick. That night I fell asleep with my face pressed against the crack of light at the bottom of the closed door.

"Do you remember that Cargill yardstick you used to have? Remember when you spanked me with it because I wouldn't sleep in my own bed?"

He glanced at me for a second, then clasped his hand hard on my knee—something he always used to do when I was little.

"You know, I didn't hit you."

"Really?"

"I sure as hell made a lot of noise though," he chuckled. "Scared the living shit out of you. Now if you have mental problems, you can blame it on me." He paused to take a long drag of his cigarette. "But I think you turned out fine. It worked too. You always slept in your own bed after that."

I wondered if he was telling me the truth. Maybe it didn't matter. He wouldn't have behaved that way if he hadn't been drunk, and the terror he instilled was traumatic enough on its own. Still, I never remembered fearing him after that, even when his fights with Mom got bad.

My mother had toughed out her marriage with an alcoholic for lots of reasons: genuine love, financial precarity, religious conviction that divorce was sin, and her belief that we were better off with a bad dad than no dad at all. By the time I was a junior in high school, I knew my dad was a drunk. When I played Hermia in the drama club's production of *A Midsummer Night's Dream*, Dad showed up on opening night drunk. Stale beer fumes hovered around him, which, based on my mother's disgust, might as well have been flies swarming putrefied meat. He didn't act drunk, only when he hugged me after curtain call did I get a whiff. "You were great up there," he said.

I was just grateful he had seen me on stage. Between the constant drinking and the construction crew job that had him on the road, I felt nearly fatherless. I clung to the tiniest crumbs of praise from him because compliments were rare and unexpected. Growing up, I'd never known how to gauge his emotions. Would he demand silence and ignore me? Become garrulous and tell funny stories? Or would he erupt in rage?

WHAT WILL OUTLAST ME?

Not long after I'd moved away to college, Mom finally filed for divorce. This was after Dad had landed a steady job at Chief Industries. He had gotten a DUI after the annual Chief Christmas party, driving home alone, when he stopped in the middle of the intersection instead of at the stop sign. Because of the DUI, his license was revoked, and he could no longer commute to Chief. He moved out and rented a dive-motel room a few blocks from the factory and bought a secondhand bicycle to get to and from work. With Dad out of the house, Mom seized the opportunity to make it permanent.

*

I saw a pickup truck approaching in the distance. Dad exchanged a one-fingered wave with the driver—a cultural norm around here.

"How's your mother?" Dad asked.

"She's fine," I said. I looked out the window at a field spotted with round hay bales. I'm sure he wondered if she was happier without him.

"We should head back," Dad said. He coughed, rattling phlegm again as he lit another cigarette. I knew he was getting antsy for a beer, ready to spend the rest of the day downing his habitual twelve-pack. He pointed the car east, toward the nearest package store in Ord, about seven miles away.

On our way, we came upon the Geranium Catholic Church, a quaint brick church with a white steeple centered on its peaked roof, a sight so familiar to me it could have been a painting over my bed. A gravel parking lot spread out in front. To its south more cornfields. Behind the church next to a small graveyard stood a life-sized crucifix.

SARAH K. LENZ

As a kindergartener, I rode with my mother every school day to meet the school bus. By driving the section line, we could intersect the bus route at the gravel lot of the church, cutting the circuitous route by ninety minutes. I remembered my fascination with the crucifix back then, with Jesus's graphically depicted agony.

Dad pulled the car to a stop. I got out. The wind lashed the gray knit skirt I was wearing, whipping it against my thighs. I headed for the statue, realizing I had never seen it up close. Rendered in black granite, Mary, Mother of Jesus, and Mary Magdalene knelt at the foot of the cross. Gazing at it, I thought about what strength it must have taken these women to watch Jesus' slow death on that cross. An anguished cry pinched Mary Magdalene's lips. Her desperate eyes gazed heavenward. I thought, I will lose my father even more slowly, like topsoil blown away by the wind. Though I'm not Catholic, I tried to remember the Hail Mary prayer, but only the last part came to me: *Holy Mary, Mother of God, pray for us sinners, now and at the hour of our death.* I liked the idea of Mary interceding for the dying, since I had been watching my father slowly kill himself for decades, poisoning his heart and lungs on a pack-a-day cigarette habit, pickling his liver with rot-gut beer. *Pray for us sinners, now.*

Dad walked up behind me. He cleared his throat and spit a ball of mucus into the tall brome grass. "Did you know we have relative buried here?" he asked.

I shook my head. He showed me my great-great grandparents' tombstone, dating back to the 1890s. I wondered why we hadn't visited the graves before, but then I realized you can only grieve what you've known.

WHAT WILL OUTLAST ME?

Neither of us had been inside the Geranium church before. It closed when I was in junior high, twenty years ago. Nailed-up plywood replaced a broken stained-glass window. Dad walked up the cement steps to the entrance and tried the door. It opened. As we crossed the vestibule into the sanctuary, a holy hush took hold. The formerly blood-red carpet was dull with dust. Hymnals and prayer books furred with cobwebs sat untouched in wooden pew racks. Light streamed in through the remaining stained glass in beams of red, green, blue, and yellow. The nave looked frozen in time.

I tried a small door to the left of the pulpit. A yellowed choir robe hung on a hook next to a small, tarnished mirror and an ancient-looking fire extinguisher. I found it oddly comforting that this safety feature was still at the ready after all these years. I caught sight of myself in the mirror and was surprised by the guilty look on my face, as if I were somehow to blame for the failures and losses that have been following my father. When I turned to leave the room, I saw Dad opening the door to the confessional, opposite the sacristy.

"I've only seen confessionals like this in the movies," he said.

"If you were Catholic," I asked, "what would you confess?"

"I wouldn't know where to begin," he said, a nervous chuckle gurgling in his tobacco-hoarsened throat.

"Okay then, if you were Catholic, who would you light a candle for?"

"Sandy," he mumbled, and turned away from me to start up the choir loft stairs.

*

When Sandy was released from the hospital in March, she was too weak to take more than a few steps at a time with her walker, even after physical therapy. Dad had wanted to take care of her, but Sandy thought she was a burden. She applied for public housing in the town where her son and grandchildren lived, two hours away from Doniphan, and moved out. Sandy was Dad's most recent loss.

I followed him up the stairs. From the choir loft, we looked down at the life-sized crucifix.

"How's Sandy doing?" I asked.

"Her mind's fuzzy," he said. "I call her every morning. We have the same conversation because she can't remember anything from the day before."

"That's too bad," I said, blinking hard against the dust motes and my own tears.

"Well, it's just the same old, same old. Same shit, different day."

On the way out of the church, we stopped in the vestibule. Dad looked up at a yellow nylon rope dangling from the belfry.

"I'll be damned," he said.

"What?"

"There's still a bell up there."

He tugged the rope. I heard a creaking like two porcelain dinner plates being rubbed together, followed by the first clap, then another.

"Sounds just like my old school bell." He grinned like a schoolboy. Encouraged, he rang it again, putting his shoulder into it this time. He tugged the rope harder and harder, letting it slide through his hands on the rebound. He kept pumping,

WHAT WILL OUTLAST ME?

but now held on tight, letting the rope pull him off the ground. He kept ringing. The sound grew louder, the rings blending into a single, unbroken pulse. My ears buzzed. I imaged the soundwaves spreading over the section lines, across the fields in concentric circles, past the Jesus statue, past the schoolhouse, past the homeplace, past Henry's Hill, spreading out wider and wider, into the universe. My father kept ringing. He was ringing away demons and thunderstorms, ringing away illnesses, ringing away random acts of God, chasing off the last heavy silences that hung between us. His grin revealed rotting teeth and beads of sweat dotted his forehead.

At last, my father let go of the rope. It took a long time for the clapper to stop. Finally, as the last reverberations faded, and Dad started to catch his breath, he began to hack and cough. I asked him if he was okay. He nodded and took a blue hanky from his back pocket, mopping his face. Then he looked at me, eyes beaming with love as dust motes swirled in a stream across the transom, snared by rays of sunlight.

SLIBNY'S FIRE

"The Slibnys' house caught fire," Mom said. She sat on the edge of my bed as I rubbed sleep from my eyes. I was only seven years old at the time, and the two older Slibny girls, Julie and Melanie, were my best friends. On the homeplace, they were our closest neighbors. Only a mile section line flanked in cornfields separated us from the Slibny's farmhouse.

"I went outside to see," Mom said. Because our farmstead was located on a hill, she could see in the distance the rolling billow of smoke, the firetrucks, and an ambulance. "I couldn't tell if the paramedics were loading anyone into the ambulance. I'm just praying everyone's okay."

It seemed incredible something so bad was happening while everything in my bedroom remained unchanged. I woke surrounded by my beloved toys: a dozen My Little Ponies neatly arranged in the stall of their two-story barn which rested against the pink wall. Next to them sat my Barbie carrying case, containing Celebration Barbie and her collection of ball gowns. Above my bed hung a Garfield the Cat poster I'd received as a free gift at my school's Scholastic book fair for buying so many Amelia Bedelia books. Mom pulled my covers back, untangling my Cabbage Patch Kid, Tallulah, from the sheets. When I saw the doll, I remembered the Cabbage Patch Kids calendar that had hung on the wall of Melanie and Julie's bedroom, and how

WHAT WILL OUTLAST ME?

the last time I'd visited them, we'd greedily pawed through each month, arguing over who's birth month had the best picture.

In retrospect, I'm surprised that my mother told me about the fire before she knew if anyone in the family had perished. I don't know how long we must have worried about their safety, nor am I certain how we found out that everyone had escaped the fire unharmed. In our small community, the fire was the most exciting thing that had happened all year. I'd eavesdropped on mom's gossipy phone conversations until I knew that the fire started in the barn in the early morning, just as Joy, Julie, and Melanie's mom, had pushed the snooze button on her alarm. The heavy smell of smoke roused her, and when she looked out the window and saw the barn, 50 yards in the distance in flames, she woke her family.

At the time of the fire, the Slibnys' house was in the process of having its foundation set, so a ring of straw bales circled it as a means of insulating the crawlspace below the house. This kept the pipes from freezing, which in the Midwest was still a threat in early March. When a gust of wind blew a spark from the barn fire to the straw bales, they ignited. In an instant the whole house was ringed in fire, and just moments later, Joy managed to shepherd her whole family—still clad in pajamas—into their aging gray station wagon from where they watched their entire house go up in a blaze.

"Burned to the ground. They lost everything." I had heard Mom said on the phone. If the gossip was to be believed, the only thing Joy saved on her way out was her purse.

After school that afternoon Dad—who had pitched in, helping the volunteer firemen until the barn and house were deemed total losses—came home to take us to see the rubble. I sat between my parents in the pickup truck cab, my knees knocking against the gearshift. Dad's truck smelled of his cigarette smoke and toasted dust blowing from the heat vent. According to my father, the fire was caused by Mr. Slibny's incompetence. The fire marshal speculated that the barn fire started when a sow with day-old piglets knocked down the heat lamp Mr. Slibny had jerry-rigged to keep her piglets warm. The lamp shattered, shooting sparks into the hay. Because of the way my father talked disparagingly about Mr. Slibny's failure to use a heat lamp properly, I assumed that bad things like this only happened to stupid people.

It was late afternoon when we pulled into the bare-dirt farmyard the Slibnys used as their driveway. Dusk cast a pale blue light over the scene. Where there had been a two-story, white clapboard farmhouse, now there was nothing but a giant pile of charred rubble. When I saw two Farmall tractors with front-loader buckets pushing and scraping at the rubble, it reminded me of scooping snow, except the color was wrong. Out of the black soot, embers glowed orange-red, like devil eyes. It reminded me of how Mrs. Ritchey, my Sunday school teacher, depicted the eternal fires of hell.

We didn't get out of the truck. Dad drove us slowly through the yard a mere 25 feet from where the house had once stood.

"What are those tractors doing, Dad?"

"They're burying it, see?"

He pointed to the mound of dirt to the west that looked like a mass grave. The tractor released its loader-bucket, dumping still smoldering pieces of house into the hole. It made a terrific sound: first cracking metal-on-metal as the bucket hinged, then the clatter of debris like giant wooden building blocks being dropped onto a cement floor.

The smell of smoke caught thick in the back of my throat. I looked at the absent space where the house had been and thought about all the things that had burnt up. Melanie and Julie's room didn't exist anymore, nor did their bunkbed, or the hardwood floor it had stood on. Even the Cabbage Patch Kid calendar and the wall it had hung on burned.

"It's a miracle they all got out safely," Mom said.

"They're lucky to be alive," Dad said.

Since then, I've often wondered at the relationship between what we call a miracle and what we deem luck. Like looking through the proverbially rose-colored glasses, faith reveals meaning to our outward reality. This is a choice the beholder must make. Was the Slibny's housefire an example of God's graciousness, sparing them death? Or was the destruction of all their possessions some sort of retribution? How hard must we look for God's love? My mom saw God, while my father thought Mr. Slibny should have known better than to set up a precarious heat lamp.

"What are the Slibnys going to do now?" Mom asked. Dad explained that the Geranium Catholic Church, the Slibnys' congregation, were taking houseware and clothing donations for the family. I never found out if the Slibnys saw their house fire as evidence of God's mercy, but perhaps their faith showed in other subtle ways that I was blind to at the time.

A few days later, my family and I went to help the Slibnys. Eventually, they would rebuild directly on the site where the old house had burned, but for the time being, they had moved into a singlewide trailer someone donated that had been hauled in and situated on top of the packed-dirt burial mound of rubble.

Before we went to visit, Mom asked me if I wanted to give Julie and Melanie anything for their new room. I settled on the Garfield poster, but I'm not sure whether selfishness or genuine friendship motivated me. It was true, of all the things in my room, the poster would be least missed, but then again, I also knew how much Melanie loved Garfield the Cat.

The trailer house shocked me. I'd never been in a home that small before. I stood awkwardly near the front door in my pink coat. The Garfield poster, rolled and clasped with a ponytail holder, hung from my fist. From that vantage, I saw the whole living area and eat-in kitchen, wall to wall brown shag carpeting, and faux wood paneling. The room was stiflingly hot. A pot of spaghetti boiled on the stove, and its starchy steam infused the whole place, condensing in thick beads on the windows.

"The girls are in their bedroom. Go on," Joy said, and made a shooing motion toward my left, where I saw a long hallway. When I reached the threshold of the bedroom, I stood there, unsure how I could enter the jumbled chaos inside. Boxes and bags of clothing stacked two or three deep lined the beaverboard walls. Mounds of clothing almost as tall me occupied the floor. It smelled like a Goodwill thrift store. Instead of a bunkbed, which would have never fit under the trailer's low ceilings anyway, the girls had new twin beds, which were engulfed by the towering piles of soft goods. I didn't see a single Barbie, Cabbage Patch Kid, or My Little Pony.

"Hi, Sarah! Look at all this stuff we have to unpack," Melanie said.

WHAT WILL OUTLAST ME?

"Wow." I nodded toward the clothes in the center of the room where Julie sat. She was sorting out which items from the huge piles to keep or give away.

"I brought you this," I said, holding the rolled poster up.

Melanie bounced Tigger-like from the bed onto a mound of clothes, and then to my spot in the hallway. When she unrolled it, she squealed in delight.

"I love Garfield! I want to put it up right above my bed." She jumped on top of the bed and stopped to stretch the poster out against the wall. I looked at it. The image depicted Garfield scratching his claws across the paper next to the words "Hang in There." As I edged into the room, shoving back the tide of clothing that had spilled into the hallway with the toe of my sneaker, I thought about how stupid it was to tell someone to just hang in there when terrible things happened. It reminded me of how whenever something bad happened to someone from church my mother said, "I'll pray for you."

Julie held up each garment she unpacked from old apple boxes and black garbage bags. "Keep or throw?" she asked. The item in question: a blouse the shade of a port-wine birthmark, like the one Jonathan, a boy from my church, had splashed across his cheek.

"What is that?" Melanie asked. There was a strange, white fabric tube tacked to the neckline.

Julie looked closer at the blouse. She determined it was a mock turtleneck collar. "This part goes around your neck," she explained.

"Gross!" Melanie said. "Throw it out." Julie wadded the disgusting shirt into a ball and lobbed it at her sister.

"No, you throw it out!" She hurled it back to Julie, who chucked it at my head. I returned her attack. We dodged the shirt like a hot potato, until out of breath, we all collapsed on a pile of clothes.

Finally, Julie put the shirt in the proper reject pile. The longer I stayed with them, the more I realized the girls were hanging in there remarkably well considering how dramatically their circumstances had changed. Was it prayers from people like my mother? The girls' faith in God? Or some strange kismet?

As I watched the system, I saw most donations were worn, stained, and smelled funny. Most people from the community were like me; they had chosen items that they didn't want or couldn't use anymore. Charity, I realized for the first time, could be sad and ugly. It wasn't simple to be like the Good Samaritan Mrs. Ritchey had told us about in Sunday school.

The following fall, the Slibnys still lived in the cramped trailer, but they'd begun construction on a new house. This house would be smaller than the one that burned, and they'd do most of the construction themselves. Rebuilding right where the old house had sat seemed its own kind of faith, like believing that lightning doesn't strike the same place twice.

That same fall my mother taught the Sunday night children's class at the Evangelical Free Church. The program, called Eager Beavers, involved a reward system for attendance, good behavior, and Bible verse memorization. The reward ribbons I coveted for their silkiness, golden embossed lettering, and rhinestones. They came in an array of rainbow colors for each level of achievement, and it took four rhinestones per ribbon to get to the next level. I was a shameless suck-up and

WHAT WILL OUTLAST ME?

teacher's pet. If I couldn't remember all of a Bible verse, I pitched a fit until my mother gave me the next rhinestone anyway.

Our church was small and most of the congregants were older, their children grown and moved away to the city. Only three kids regularly attended: Jonathan, his cousin Nicole, and me. Eager Beavers was held in the church basement, which smelled like the mildew that clung to its cinderblock walls. Pastor Ritchey led the opening singing. His basso profundo clashed with our childishly high voices as we sang our theme song: "We are Eager Beavers working for the Lord. Yes, we are Eager Beavers!" Afterwards Mrs. Ritchey brought snacks, usually triangle-shaped baloney sandwiches on day-old bread and watery grape Kool-Aid.

"Next week, if you bring a friend, you get double Beaver Builder points, and two extra rhinestones on your ribbon!" Mom announced at the end of class. This was a proselytizing effort on her part. If new kids came, she could tell them the truth about Jesus.

Mom suggested that I invite Melanie Slibny even though she'd just had her first holy communion at the Geranium Catholic Church. Mom and I had spent a lot of time waiting in the church's parking lot, which was also my school bus stop. As we sat in the car, I thought about Jesus a lot because in the cemetery next to the church stood a life-size crucifix.

I'd asked Jesus into my heart the year before, as a kindergartener. Under the prompting of Mrs. Ritchey, my Sunday school teacher, I had recited the words of the Sinner's Prayer in the belief that admitting my sins and asking Jesus into my heart would save me from the fires of hell because he had died on the cross for my sins and then rose again into heaven. One morning waiting for the bus, as I looked out the car window, I pondered Jesus. "If Jesus rose from the dead, then why is he still on the cross?" I asked Mom.

"It's because Catholics don't believe the same things about Jesus that we do," she replied.

It puzzles me now to think about this theological hairsplitting. At the E-Free Church, we were taught that anyone who hadn't asked Jesus into their heart through repeating the Sinners' Prayer was going to hell. But what about Melanie's experience during Holy Communion? Weren't these two different rituals with the same spirit of humility, faith, and acceptance of Jesus?

The next Sunday night, I knocked on the trailer house's frail aluminum door, and when Joy opened it, the aroma of sauerkraut hit my nostrils, pungent and sharp. Melanie swished on her nylon windbreaker. It was purple and teal. She grabbed her Bible. I was surprised that it was exactly like mine, a white, Precious Moments edition.

We sat in the backseat. Dad drove us, and Mom sat in front with him. I showed Melanie my favorite Eager Beaver Award ribbon that I used as a bookmark in my Bible. It was pink with four rhinestones. We flipped through the illustrated pages in our Bibles and bickered over which picture we thought was best. I liked the toe-headed shepherd because I thought he looked kind with his round, doe eyes, and because the sheep he held reminded me of my kittens, which I adored. Melanie argued that the angel picture was best.

"Look, the angel has a halo and angels watch over you and protect you. Angels are better than shepherds," she said.

WHAT WILL OUTLAST ME?

"Well angels aren't better than Jesus," I said. I racked my brain for something Mrs. Ritchey had told me about angels. "Satan was an angel once," I said.

In reply Melanie lurched forward with her head between her knees and vomited. Her puke plopped against the car's floorboard. I slid across the slick vinyl into the far corner of the backseat to get away from it, but I couldn't take my eyes off it. Shreds of sauerkraut splashed on the car's black floor mat. Grayish bits—what must have been pork roast—came up next. In between her heaves, I realized Melanie was crying. Mom turned from the front seat and began patting her back as she continued to vomit. Melanie stopped just as Dad pulled the car over, then flipped a U-turn on the desolate highway. Our old Plymouth sailed over the hills. Melanie sat whimpering. I tried not to gag at the smell. I saw that some vomit had fallen on the seat. She tried to spread her legs to avoid it, but on the slick vinyl seats, she couldn't. Her stonewashed jeans soon darkened where she sat. Her feet straddled the larger puddle on the floor.

"It's okay. You'll be home soon," Mom said.

"Roll the windows down," Dad said. "We need air." He tromped on the accelerator. I pinned myself to the far back corner of the bench seat, as far from the vomit as I could manage.

When we arrived back at the trailer, Joy came out immediately when she heard the dog bark at our car. She must have been doing dishes when we arrived because she was still drying her hands with a kitchen towel. When Melanie stumbled out of the car, Joy's eyes widened the moment she saw the accident.

"Oh my gosh, I'm so sorry. She didn't tell me she wasn't feeling well." Joy took the dish towel and began wiping the backseat. I watched in amazement as she used her towel and bare hands.

Mom told her not to worry about it. She said we were planning on having the Plymouth's carpet shampooed anyway, which I knew was a lie. Then almost as quickly as we'd sailed back to Melanie's house, we left again, worried now, that we'd be late for Eager Beavers.

I shivered against my jacket and squinted as the wind blew the stray pieces of hair that had escaped my pigtails into my eyes. "I'm cold," I whined, but Mom and Dad decided cold was better than the acrid smell of throw up.

When we got to the church, it was dismal as always. Jonathan had brought his friend Brian, a weird kid wearing horn-rimmed glasses. After we sang the Eager Beaver song with Pastor Ritchey, my mother stood up and awarded Jonathan a new, pale blue ribbon with two rhinestones. I felt hot tears building up behind my eyes at the unfairness of it all. I didn't have a blue ribbon yet. By the time Pastor Ritchey dismissed us to our classroom, and I sat down in my usual teacher's pet spot up front, the hot tears had escalated to real sobs.

"It's not fair," I wailed, interrupting the beginning of Mom's lesson. I wouldn't calm down, so finally, she said, "Fine. You can have a blue ribbon, too." Jonathan and Brian stared at me but didn't say anything.

"Lord knows you tried to bring a friend," Mom said as she handed over the coveted blue ribbon. Later in the class, Jonathan and I watched as Brian recited the Sinner's Prayer with my mother, just as Mrs. Ritchey had done with me and Jonathan.

We never invited any of the Slibnys to church again, nor did we ever make another attempt to proselytize. I'm not sure why we dropped the evangelistic efforts. Years later I still wonder about that night. Now it seems arrogant to think that anyone who doesn't experience God exactly the way I do is lost, or that salvation boils down to repeating one rote prayer. There is something about spiritual conversion experiences, too, that remain mysteriously private. How can anyone ever truly know the spirit with which one confesses or prays? Maybe Melanie getting sick that night had saved her from a fundamental religion that did more harm than good. Maybe Melanie hadn't needed saving at all.

The next spring the Slibnys moved into their new house. The girls' bedrooms were in the unfinished basement. On my first visit to the new house, Melanie proudly showed me the Garfield poster, which somehow, she'd managed to stick to the damp cinderblock wall with chunks of sticky-tac putty. "Thank you," she said.

"For what?" I asked.

"Don't you remember? You gave it to me."

I'd forgotten such a menial thing, but she'd cherished it enough to put it up in her new bedroom. For her the poster had been a special token of kindness, something that she truly liked among all that unloved secondhand clothing. I felt guilty that I hadn't given her something more and wished I were that grateful. It took me many years after this to realize that gratitude was another way to see the world as full of God's love.

I looked at the narrow window at the top of the wall by her bed. It was much too narrow for a person to slip through, and I noticed that there was no fire escape in the basement. I didn't say anything. Melanie had already been saved by fire once. Who's to say she wouldn't be saved again? Perhaps we're all saved over and over again, but most of the time we fail to see it because we can't comprehend the divine providence behind it. As for sleeping every night in a basement without a fire escape, that seemed like a kind of faith to me as well—an unwavering conviction that things work out exactly the way they're meant to.

LIGHTNING FLOWERS

A trio of open caskets is propped on wooden straight back chairs. The open lids of each white coffin reveal a square peephole framing the face and torso of three dead bodies. On top of the caskets, shiny placards read in ornate scroll: "At Rest." Like all corpses laid out for funeral rites, the three boys exude a certain peacefulness due to the careful closing of their eyes and mouth, what morticians call "setting the features." The dead brothers wear matching dark suits and black bowties. Their dark hair is slicked back from their foreheads. Carnations rest on their chests, near clasped hands. Edgar Allen Poe in triplicate, I think, but I can't tell if it's the hair, the dark suits, or the morbid situation that brings this to mind. In the background, a ladder-shaped shadow that the wooden chairs make and the white curtains of the parlor take on the blur of an apparition. In the foreground, the bottoms of the caskets are cropped out of the photo. The coffins slant toward the viewer at a precarious angle, as if at the slightest stirring each casket could slip, topple to the ground, and spill its contents.

*

My father gave me the photograph. I was visiting him in central Nebraska. I hadn't seen him in over a year. He looked older than I remembered, the sagging skin around his eyes more pronounced, the hair around his temples whiter. Almost a decade after his divorce from my mother, he had started to rid his house of clutter and memorabilia—things he thinks he won't need for the rest of his life—as he plans on moving into public housing for senior citizens.

"I've got something for you," he said. He took me to the back bedroom and dug through the closet. "Here, you're the family historian. You should have this."

He handed me the framed photograph lacquered with dust. Flecks of molded plaster decorating the frame crumbled when I touched it. I'd seen this photo before, heard the story: they were struck by lightning. But looking at it was still chilling.

I'm not sure why this photograph haunts me. Though they are my great uncles, I can't call them my "dearly departed." They died nearly 100 years ago, and anyone who would have known them is dead now too. I am certain this is the only extant photograph of these relatives. They have ceased to live on in any memory. What remains is a 10 x 12 silver gelatin print.

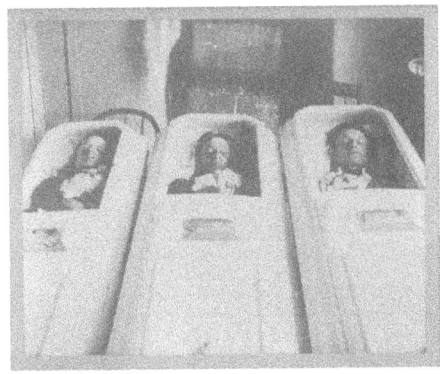

After my dad gave me the picture, I put it face down on the backseat of my car. The next day, I drove to Lincoln to visit my cousin, Erin. From there I would drive home to Ohio.

WHAT WILL OUTLAST ME?

When I arrived at Erin's ranch-style suburban house, she was just as I remembered. Petite, blonde, and wearing too much blue eye shadow. I hadn't seen her in two years, not since my sister's wedding, but growing up we had been as close as sisters. Erin's mom, my aunt Dixie, died of breast cancer when Erin was six and I was seven. Our aunts made sure Dixie's legacy lived on by mothering Erin as their own and telling her as many stories about Dixie as they could remember.

Erin had given birth to a premature baby who died five years ago. Though she is only nine months younger than me, Erin's life has been transformed by these tragic deaths in ways I cannot imagine. I have gotten this far without a death in the immediate family. But it's only a matter of time.

I brought Erin a bottle of Patrón. We sat at the kitchen table drinking shots of tequila chased by Diet Coke. We talked about the aunts. Counting Dixie and my mother, Carollee, there are six aunts, and three have been ravaged in varying degrees by breast cancer. My mom, though now in remission, has had breast cancer twice. The second time it returned even after her double mastectomy. Another aunt, Beth, is dying of stage IV breast cancer. It has metastasized to her bones.

"I was supposed to get a mammogram this year," Erin told me because she had turned 30, and she and I are both high risk. "My mom was our age when she was diagnosed. What was it that gave them all cancer?" she asked.

"I don't know," I said. I told Erin about how I got a mammogram last year because I'd found a lump, but it was benign. After my breasts had been X-rayed, the doctor showed me the images: veins and masses, circles of cysts some benign, maybe others not. Smashed into two-dimensional, amoeba-like blobs glowing on the screen, my breasts seemed no longer a part of me, but something primordial with blossoming capillary trails in electric blue.

"More tequila?" I asked.

Erin nodded. We raised our glasses, slammed back the liquor, and sucked on wedges of lime, dulling the alcohol's fire.

Later, because we were talking about death and I was a bit drunk, I told Erin about my corpse photograph. "I want to see it," she said.

I ran across her manicured front lawn and got the photo from my car. When I came back I felt bashful about showing it to her. Though she wanted to see it, the image felt petty or oversensationalized, like rubbernecking. We can't help looking at the scene of an accident, but why does it rivet us? Maybe it makes us grateful we are still alive. Maybe it shows us what we don't want to imagine: what death—when it finally comes for us—may be like.

Back in the kitchen, I put the framed photograph on the table.

"You're right, that's creepy," Erin said. "But Ayden's photographs don't bother me at all. I'll show you." She fetched a blue gingham baby book.

I only know the roughest outline of what she had experienced with Ayden. He had been born premature and he died. "How long did he live?" I asked her.

"Five months." Then she told me how he was on life support the entire time, but finally the doctors had told her and her husband that Ayden's organs were going to start shutting

WHAT WILL OUTLAST ME?

down. They could either keep him on the breathing tubes or let him go peacefully.

I flipped open the album. Many of the photos had been carefully contrived. I noticed Ayden looks like his oldest brother, who had also been born premature, but survived and is now a 5th grader. Preemie Ayden is fragile, inchoate, and wrinkled. His chapped skin is never quite the right color—sometimes jaundiced yellow, sometimes ashen gray. Always a respirator tube connects to his mouth, taped in place like a small, clear vacuum hose. IV needles pierce his skin and tubes curl from his body in every direction like tentacles.

These posed photos speak to the desire of the beholder. On Easter, Ayden is staged with a stuffed plush rabbit and an Easter basket. On another occasion, he wears a camouflaged hat that reads: "Daddy's Little Hunter." Erin and her husband had hired a professional photographer to take a family portrait: detailed close ups of Ayden's chapped feet, captured in artistic black and white. The families of infants in the Neonatal Intensive Care Unit are encouraged to take photos. Memorializing infants with only a tenuous grip on life gives the small soul a history and a story. Erin had painstakingly documented Ayden's existence, proving for a moment he had been a member of her family, her beloved son. Photographs are witnesses, affirming we lived, and our lives made a difference. This urge to accumulate evidence shouldn't be surprising now that we digitally document and timeline our lives on social media, but it goes further than that. We remember the dead because we want to be remembered too.

In 2005, a mother who had lost her six-day old baby to a rare congenital disorder started the nonprofit Now I Lay Me Down to Sleep. The organization enlists the volunteer services of 1,500 professional photographers to photograph babies like Ayden around the US and in forty different countries. These pro bono shutterbugs photograph babies in the NIC-U both before and after they die. The website advertising copy—aimed at would-be volunteer photographers— reads, "Capture special moments of love for parents experiencing the loss of an infant. Your precious gift provides healing for a family while honoring the baby's legacy." Now I Lay Me Down to Sleep calls their services remembrance photography, which is considered an integral tool in the parents' grieving process.

Photographing children postmortem is not new. From the 1850s and into the late 1920s, millions of postmortem photographs were shot, depicting deceased of every demographic. The convergence of more affordable and accessible daguerreotypes (and, later, silver emulsion prints) and reliable embalming techniques developed during the American Civil War, coupled with a high mortality rate, led to the popularity of postmortem images. Postmortems then went out of fashion during the Great Depression as people began to consider them morbid and vulgar.

The postmortem images of Ayden are beautiful. Only after his death does he look like a healthy baby. Thanks to a skillful mortician's makeup job, Ayden's skin appears smooth and rosy. "He looks just like he's sleeping," I told Erin when I saw the first postmortem photograph of him. She said, "I love looking at him without the tubes."

*

When I got back home to Ohio, I contacted my old photography instructor to ask him about the coffin portrait. I thought he might see something in the photograph I had

WHAT WILL OUTLAST ME?

missed. Gil works at the Rutherford B. Hayes Presidential Museum in Fremont, and he recommended I contact the rare manuscripts curator there, a woman named Nan Card.

"Nan is the resident death gal at the museum," he told me over the phone.

When I met Nan a few days later and told her this, she chuckled in a raspy cigarette-hardened voice. We sat and chatted in her messy office, the desk between us piled with files, papers, and books.

"Let me show you what I brought," I said as I handed her the coffin portrait. She scanned it appreciatively.

"I collected postmortems," Nan said. "But when my grandson was born, I took all the death pictures down. I didn't want him seeing them."

Nan handed me a book, a limited-edition monograph entitled *Sleeping Beauty: Memorial Photography in America*. In 1990, Dr. Stanley Burns released this collection of postmortems. Nan's assistant walked in, wheeling a cart of acid-free archive boxes. "Oh," she said, shuddering. "That book gives me nightmares."

Nan showed me to the reading room and introduced me to the head librarian, who took down the names of my great uncles: Johnnie, Charlie, and Lumir Krahulik. When I was in Nebraska, Dad had taken me to see their grave. The only date carved on the white marble tombstone had been the year: 1914. The librarian disappeared into her cubicle to try to find their obituary in a digital archive. I settled in at a reading table with the corpse portrait next to me.

"Oh, my word," Gil said when he came over to see the photo. The dead faces in the photo are the most disturbing.

"Those are burn marks, right?" I asked of the dark smudges around the corpses' faces, "not just flaws in the photograph?"

Gil took out his loupe. "Yep, they're roughed up quite good."

I looked through the magnifying lens and saw burn marks splayed across the boys' chins. A deep gash cuts across the lip of the oldest boy. They probably aren't cuts at all, but lightning flowers or Lichtenberg figures, named after the German physicist who in 1777 studied the patterns high voltage static electricity made. When a current of lightning passes through the skin, capillaries rupture and bloom into fernlike burns underneath. Like tributaries, they mark the flow of the stream, a heart-stopping volt of electricity.

"How did you say they were killed?" Gil asked.

"They were getting the horses in from a storm when they were struck by lightning. They were all killed instantly, and the barn burnt to the ground."

Gil left me to look at the *Sleeping Beauties*. As I turned the pages, I noticed each photo had something that caught my eye, and that, like the burned faces of my great uncles, made me uneasy. In "Mother Holds Daughter with Rigor Mortis While Father Mourns" (1846) it was the awkward, rigidly straight arms of the dead girl. In "Child Dead from Dehydration due to Intestinal Disease" (1854), it was the child's sunken cheeks contrasted with her bulbous, skeletal head. In "Charlie—a Boy with his Toys" (1850), it was the deceased's half open eyes gazing longingly at the wagon he'll never play with again.

WHAT WILL OUTLAST ME?

French theorist Roland Barthes has a word for details like this: *punctum*. Like the period under an exclamation point, a sharp needle prick, the hole an arrow makes, or the spot where lightning strikes, *punctum* is a detail that attracts or distresses the viewer. The *punctum* can arouse sympathy or a flash of insight. Barthes explains in *Camera Lucida*, "However lightning-like it may be, the *punctum* has...a power of expansion. This power if often metonymic." For Barthes, photographs could transcend themselves, becoming no longer the medium, the stand-in representing reality, but reality itself. He asks, "Is this not the sole proof of its art?"

Like referents to Madonna and Child, the mothers in these antique postmortem photos cradle their dead children. But unlike da Vinci or Raphael Madonnas with beatific expressions, these mothers are stoic. In the daguerreotype of "Mother Holding her Dead Child" (1855), the woman meets the gaze of the camera straight on, jaw set firm, as if her stony countenance could prevent an emotional breakdown.

Erin's pictures with Ayden are different. In the photo that haunts me the most, Erin holds Ayden in an upright position, sitting on her lap facing her, so his back is turned to the camera. For a minute it's easy to believe he's a normal infant because the tubes that spider across his face, enter his rosebud mouth, and snake down his tiny nose aren't in sight. The *punctum* is Erin's eyes. They are full of tears. The pain in her red-rimmed eyes seems so private, that I had gasped the first time I saw it.

"What?" Erin had asked. In that moment I had felt like I crossed a boundary, overstepped a line of decency.

"This is such a…" I hadn't known what to say. "It feels…" Then I managed tell her, "Somehow this picture snatches your emotions. Don't you feel like this photo violates your privacy?"

"That was the day," Erin said, "we took Ayden off life support. I love that picture because I loved the back of his little head and wanted a picture of it." Erin is deeply religious. I realize that gives her strength. She is certain Dixie and Ayden are in heaven together, waiting for the rest of the family to join them. I am awed by her nonchalance. She's had several years to process this grief, but even so, I'm struck by her unselfishness. She's given the viewer a gift: raw emotion. This snapshot is the antithesis of a Kodak moment. It documents not a birthday party or wedding, the sort of event that we normally want to relive in memory, but a point in time no one would ever want to go through once, let alone over again in memory. This photo of Erin's face contorted in sorrow allows viewers to experience, at a deeply personal level, a horror not their own.

Kafka said, "We photograph things in order to drive them out of our minds." If he is right, postmortem photographs are a way of shelving grief so we don't have to confront it again and again. Having trapped the gruesome face of death, relegated it to a closed photo album, pain fades. The emulsion of chemicals on light-sensitive paper remembers so we don't have to.

*

The librarian came back to my table with a piece of paper. "I'm sorry. There's no digital copy of the newspaper that printed their obituary," she told me. "But I did find this." She handed me a printout of the 1910 census record listing the boys and their brother, Rudolph, my great grandfather. From this I pieced together how old they had been when they died. Charlie

WHAT WILL OUTLAST ME?

was 15, Lumir 13, and Johnnie 11. The librarian also gave me an index listing the boys' death notice published on May 28th, 1914.

"Their obituaries are probably only available on microfilm," she explained.

Later I called the Ord Township Library, the library of my childhood, and asked how I could access the obituaries from out of state.

"Tell me the dates and names again," Diane the librarian said over the phone. I did, and she said, "Wait, are you Carollee's daughter?"

"Yes."

"How's your mom doing?"

I didn't want to answer. I didn't know this woman and was taken aback by her personal question. Ord was such a small town that I realized Diane had probably gone to my mom's cancer benefit dinner to raise money for her medical bills. Did she want to know if my mom was still in remission? It was none of her business, I thought.

"She's well," I said and left it at that. Even though my mom's been pronounced cancer-free, we knew it could strike again.

*

When I told my mother about the postmortem photography I was researching, she surprised me by saying, "Oh, I have photos of Grandpa B at his funeral. Your uncle took them."

She agreed to send them to me. These postmortems of grandpa would be different than photographs of dead strangers.

Harder to look at, I thought. When the envelope arrived in the mail, I waited months before I felt ready to open it.

I had attended grandpa's funeral as a middle schooler. At the visitation before the funeral, my cousins, Erin and Brian, had dared me to touch the body because we were all a bit terrified of grandpa's corpse. When I finally worked up the courage to touch it, my dead grandfather's hand had felt like grandma's Naugahyde couch: smooth, cool, and synthetic. "I bet his bald head feels like a bowling ball," Brian had said with a smirk. I don't think Brian ever tested his theory. Soon after that we left the funeral parlor's slumber room to climb trees in the landscaping across the street. We were old enough to know better, but brazen enough not to care, trying to do something that would take our minds off death.

I had won the dare but felt anything but triumphant. What I felt was defeat, was grief. Undertaker Thomas Lynch writes about exactly this type of schizophrenia in his memoir, *The Undertaking: Life Studies from the Dismal Trade*. "We are drawn to the dead and yet abhor them, grief places them on pedestals and buries them in graves. We love and hate them all at once." For Lynch, funerals and graveyards "seek to mend these gaps between our fears and our fond feelings, between the sickness and the sadness it variously awakens in us, between the weeping and dancing [or tree climbing] we are driven to" when someone we love dies.

In every corpse I've seen there's been something—off. The mortician can lacquer and paint, position limbs and facial features just so, but he can't make us forget that it's not really our loved one but an inanimate husk. With grandpa it had been his mouth. In life he had an under bite, and his lower lip always

WHAT WILL OUTLAST ME?

stuck out a bit. In death his lips had been clamped into a thin line I didn't recognize. When I finally opened the packet of snapshots taken of grandpa at his funeral, I was surprised by the things I remembered from fifteen years ago—like the strange set of his mouth—but also by the things I had forgotten, like his liver-spotted hands or the color of the flowers on the casket.

A few months after Grandpa passed away, my great uncle Joe died, and though I barely knew him, my parents had made me go to the funeral. On Uncle Joe's corpse, his hands had been distorted. Because he'd loved to fish, Joe was buried holding a fishing reel. Under the recessed lighting of the funeral parlor, he had looked waxy, while the metallic reel was animated by the light sparkling on its shiny surface. His fingers looked boneless. Where knuckles should have been, the unbroken line of smooth flesh stretched like giant linguine noodles.

When Uncle Joe's son drove his father's fishing boat behind the hearse on the way to the cemetery, it had been too much for my mother.

"That's so stupid. His boat's not going to go with him," she had whispered to me as we stood at the graveside. Her concept of heaven didn't include fishing rods or aluminum boats with outboard motors. Whether it had been Uncle Joe's wife's idea or his grown children's, someone imagined Joe would be fishing in heaven.

*

Diane at the Ord Township Library had agreed to look up the microfilm herself and transcribe the obituary for me. I didn't think this was protocol but a kindness she had bestowed on me because she knew my mother. The day after we spoke on the phone I received an email with the obituary. "THREE

BROTHERS IN ONE GRAVE," the headline read. The obituary recounted how their father, Frank, had returned from town, and the boys were untacking his four-horse team. "The storm came up and their mother urged them to come in the house but they preferred to remain in the barn, telling their mother that they would come in after the storm," the article read. Charlie had just returned home from business college four days before, and I imagined the brothers were catching up, telling stories, and joking privately. Had they been in awe of the storm? Had they stopped to ponder the majestic thunderheads, clouds the color of pewter? Why hadn't they listened to their mother? Had she nagged them too much already that day? The obituary goes on: "They were standing in the doorway of the barn watching the rain. The flash came and Mrs. Krahulik, remembering her sons, looked to the barn and saw a flame. She and her husband then rushed to the barn and found the three lifeless bodies."

By a stroke of luck, my great grandfather, 17 at the time, was spared. Like me, the obit writer had speculated, "Rudolph, an older boy, also living at home, was at the time at the home of his sister, Mrs. John Beran Jr., helping care for her sick infant. This circumstance no doubt saved him. Had he been home, he would doubtless have been with the other boys." My grandfather, my father, and I were but a lightning strike from existing. Probability played its part. In the US between 1910 and 1919, out of every million people, between four and five were killed by lightning. Irrespective of circumstances (standing in the doorway of large building during a thunderstorm), odds of any three people together being struck by lightning in 1914 were just under one in ten thousand trillion.

WHAT WILL OUTLAST ME?

The odds of my getting breast cancer are much higher. One out of eight American women, or 12 percent, will be diagnosed with the disease in their lifetime. With a family history like mine, researchers speculate I may have up to a 72 percent risk of being diagnosed with breast cancer. Will a cluster of malignant cells darken the screen of my next mammogram? Will cancer bloom in bright, healthy tissue? I worry too about my mother. Will her cancer come back a third time? Her doctors tell her there's a 10 percent chance her tumor will reoccur. She's prepared. She's even told me what music she wants at her funeral.

But there will be no postmortem photos, no *momento mori* of any kind. Mom wouldn't want them, nor will I need them. When the time comes, I'll remember her from the hundreds of snapshots collected in scrapbooks and albums. Postmortem photographs are partly a response to scarcity, when few other records existed to remember loved ones by, either because portraits and photography were expensive and time-consuming (as in the case of my uncles), or because, like Ayden, the deceased didn't live long enough to be their subject.

Postmortem photographs keep the thought of death near. Montaigne believed the key to living well meant dwelling on death. "Let us have nothing on our minds as often as death," he wrote. "At every moment let us picture it in our imaginations in all its aspects." I used to think that *memento mori* meant "remember the dead," and assumed that was the purpose of postmortem photography. But when I recently looked up the phrase I found its literal translation from the Latin far less congenial: *Remember that you will die.*

SARAH K. LENZ

 Through small but continual reminders of death, we live more fully and waste less of the precious time we have to spend among the living. The purpose of postmortem photographs isn't just to remember the dead, but to remind us that—though soon enough we too will die—for the time being we are still alive.

SHOOTING ON IZARD STREET

"Have you ever been the victim of a violent crime?" he asked.

It was a simple enough question, yet I hesitated. I sat in the jury box at the Baldwin County Courthouse in Milledgeville, Georgia, where I'd recently moved from the Midwest. The faces around me reflected the racial demographic of the Deep South, equally split between white and black. As the prosecuting attorney posed the question to each of the other eleven people called up for jury selection, I thought about the time fifteen years ago, when I'd seen a man in my neighborhood die of gunshot wounds. Since my personal property had been damaged, my vehicle left riddled with bullet holes, I decided, yes, I'd been a victim. My response granted me release from serving on that jury, but as I walked home from the courthouse that day, I wondered if I had been entirely honest under oath. Being a witness to a violent crime is not the same as being a victim.

*

The shooting happened the summer before 9/11. I lived in an efficiency apartment in midtown Omaha on 33rd and Izard Street. After getting kicked out of Grace College of the Bible for unchristian behavior (smoking cigarettes), I'd transferred to the state university. At twenty years old I was in that phase my mother called "being wild." Though I was in college on a PELL grant and got good grades, I experimented with drugs and had sex with whomever I wanted.

Before I moved to Izard Street, I'd been crashing with friends in a party house since the dorms had closed after spring semester finals. I moved out the day after I was almost raped by my housemate's brother. Luckily, he was more inebriated than me that night, which had given me just enough speed and strength to fight him off. I found the tiny apartment in the *Omaha World-Herald* want ads, rented it on the spot, and paid the deposit with a thick stack of fives, tens, and ones—tips from my waitressing job at Chili's.

The apartment's distinguishing features were a narrow bathroom built awkwardly underneath a stairwell, a kitchen smaller than most closets, and a cockroach problem. It was close to my university, but because it was also near North Omaha, the notoriously crime-ridden part of the city where few white people lived, its rent was low. I took comfort in the fact the apartment was just a few blocks from the Walnut Hill neighborhood, known for its large parks and restored Victorian mansions. Even if this is an iffy neighborhood, I thought, it's the best I can afford. Living at the party house that was cheaper but made me feel unsafe wasn't an option now. My parents lived paycheck to paycheck themselves, so I knew I couldn't ask them for money.

The week I moved in, I drove back to my parents' home in central Nebraska so I could borrow my dad's red Mazda pickup to move some furniture. Jay, a Chili's co-worker, helped me move in. He looked remarkably like Shaquille O'Neil, I noticed

WHAT WILL OUTLAST ME?

as we sat across from each other on the twin bed we'd just carried in, passing a joint. He didn't own a car, so I gave him a ride home that night. He lived with his mother in a run-down HUD house in North Omaha. After that night we spent a lot of time at my apartment. I liked his quiet, calm demeanor. It made me feel safe around him. Jay was a sophomore elementary education major and wanted to be a kindergarten teacher. He was the polar opposite of the drunk, arrogant white guys my old roommates befriended. He was funny too. He played Afroman's song "Because I Got High" for me, and we cracked up at the lyrics. We smoked pot because it was cheaper than alcohol and easier to get when you're underage. We bought from Jay's twin brother Footy, who made his living selling weed. Marijuana made working our shit-jobs more bearable. It also made us lascivious, so after a couple of smoke out sessions at my apartment, one thing led to another and we slept together, and then we agreed that neither of us would sleep with anyone else. Jay and I fell into a habit of spending our free afternoons and evenings getting high and having sex at my apartment. We worked as many shifts as we could, so there'd be money for school that financial aid didn't cover.

*

One lazy summer afternoon shortly after Jay and I started dating, we were in a car accident on Izard Street. It was my fault. I pulled out from my parallel parking space without checking my blind spot just as a car drove by. The car sheered into my front fender, plowing a large dent in it. The other car's front tire popped at the impact. It was a Lexus, painted a silvery-beige that the driver would tell the cop was called champagne when he filled out the accident report. The Lexus also sported a vanity plate: MGM GOLF.

Just as I opened my door to examine the damage, Mr. MGM trotted toward me, face red.

"Didn't you fucking see me?" he said. I noticed a gold watch on his wrist, and he came close enough that I could smell his Calvin Klein cologne. I was scared. Behind me Jay emerged from the passenger side. Standing six foot-four on the grassy curb, he towered above the roof of the car. As soon as Mr. MGM saw Jay, his demeanor changed instantly.

"I'm sorry," he mumbled, and I saw fear flicker across his face. He was afraid of Jay.

"I'm going to call the cops and just wait over here." He pulled out his cell phone and gestured to the other side of the street, closer to his car.

"Did ya see that?" Jay said. I nodded. "He looked like he thought I was going to pull a gun on him."

At the time, I didn't think much of it. Of course Jay was intimidating because he's so tall. But now I think Mr. MGM was probably reacting more to Jay's skin color than anything else. Though the man could have lived in one of the Victorian mansions just a few blocks from my street, he seemed far enough out of his element to be genuinely afraid. The whole scene could have escalated out of control if Jay had done anything perceived as violent. At the time it didn't register that fear and misunderstanding might quickly turn deadly for a black man. I was grateful Jay had diffused another man's anger. Just by his presence, by the way he so easily evoked fear, he'd protected me.

WHAT WILL OUTLAST ME?

A police officer arrived on the scene and questioned all three of us. When the cop saw it was a straightforward error on my part of refusing to yield the right-of-way, he wrote me a moving violation ticket. When he tried to call a tow truck, Mr. MGM refused. Instead he popped open his trunk, removed an expensive-looking set of golf clubs so he could get the spare, and changed the flat faster than I've seen anyone change a tire.

The next time cops were called to Izard Street that summer, the situation was violent. Jay and I were lounging on the window seat overlooking the backyard's sickly patch of lawn and a few mulberry trees. The apartment was hot and sticky in the July afternoon. I wore only a bra and panties. From his spot next to me, Jay, clad in his boxer shorts, passed me his glass pipe. He'd packed it with primo hydroponic pot. I had just taken a hit, letting the thick stream of smoke slowly escape from my lungs, when we heard it: a deafening crack followed by a loud volley of pops. At first, I thought the sound was fireworks, until Jay grabbed my arm and yelled, "Get down. Gunshots!"

We flopped to the floor belly first. Grit and lint from the worn carpet stuck to my sweat-damp skin and began to itch.

"What do we do?" I crawled around the bed, looking for my jeans.

"We wait." He gestured to the windows, from where stray bullets might fly. I peeked out the window but couldn't see anything. After about five minutes, Jay told me that whoever had fired that shot was probably long gone, having fled the scene. He stood up and slowly pulled his red polo with the Chili's pepper logo stitched on it over his head. With trembling hands, I got dressed too. We smelled like sweat, sex, and stale tortilla chips.

    We cautiously walked up the sidewalk, around to the front of the house. That's when we saw the police. Two men in riot gear crouched behind my dad's red Mazda truck parked on the street. Their captain gave an all-clear. They hustled, still crouching, to the lawn across the street where a Black man laid face-up on the grass.

    Officers strung up yellow police tape, zigzagging from the perimeter of my front yard to the victim's front yard, blocking off Izard Street. One cop stood still behind the police line in the center of the street. His dark face looked ashy. A team of EMTs arrived by ambulance and helped the officer onto a stretcher. Later, the newspaper said he'd been hit in the leg by a piece of metal ricocheting off a nearby parked vehicle. It didn't realize the man lying on the grass was dead until I saw how the EMTs ignored him. From where Jay and I stood behind the police-line tape, I couldn't see the man's face. The only detail I made out was his dark blue JNCO jeans, familiar to me because that was Footy, Jay's twin brother's, favorite brand.

    I wondered how much blood seeped into the grass. This body was the center around which the whole scene swirled, charged with a negative energy. Like pressing the wrong sides of magnets together, I felt repulsed, yet fixed in my spot, wanting to both run back to the safety of my apartment, and to duck under the police tape so I could take a closer look at the body.

    A Channel 7 News van screeched to a stop along 34th street. A news anchor and cameraman ran out, only to be shooed back like geese by another cop. The whole block teemed with blue-uniformed officers.

WHAT WILL OUTLAST ME?

The Asian lady who lived in the apartment next to mine, and the Black man from upstairs who I occasionally sold small amounts of weed to, joined us on the lawn.

"What happened?" the Asian lady asked.

"That man got shot," I said.

"He's dead," the Black man said.

"He probably on drugs."

Jay stayed quiet.

Then I noticed a face in the upstairs window across the street. A small child, about four years old stared down at us with blank eyes. Later I'd find out from reading the newspaper that the man dead in the grass was that little boy's stepfather.

"Look. In that upstairs window," I said.

"Poor kid," Jay said, "I bet he saw the whole thing."

"Why doesn't somebody help him?"

Jay shrugged back at me. It wasn't our habit for me to be the one asking the questions. Usually, he was the one that grilled me. Sometimes he felt more like an annoying younger sibling than my lover.

A policeman came and took statements from Jay and me, though we couldn't tell him much, only that we heard the shots, and didn't come out of the apartment until all the shooting was over. After he wrote down my statement I asked, "Do things like this happen a lot in this neighborhood? I just moved here."

"Miss," he said, "a shooting can happen anywhere."

Soon after I gave my statement, a tow truck arrived and began chaining up the red truck. "Hey!" I yelled from behind the police line. "Why are they taking my vehicle?" The officer who had interviewed me slowly walked back to me. "We're taking the vehicle as evidence. We have to extract the bullets from it."

Though I was upset about the truck being impounded, that anger faded when I realized I had a legitimate excuse to call off for the dinner shift. Jay, deciding he needed the money more than a night off, caught a bus to his evening shift at Chili's.

It was dark by the time the police left. The man's body laid on the grass for hours before the coroner made his examination, packed the corpse into a body bag, and wheeled it away on a gurney. Finally, the police tape was rolled up, and the street returned to normal. No trace of what had happened remained.

The next morning, I unfolded the *World-Herald*, to find the front page devoted to the shooting on Izard Street. According to the newspaper, the events leading to the shooting of Willie Greenlow started when his wife Dwanessa called 911. "My husband is shooting. My four-year-old is still in the house," she told the dispatcher. When seven officers arrived nine minutes later and knocked on the door, allegedly the response was a bullet through a window. Officers took cover behind a retaining wall and my dad's red truck. When Greenlow burst out the front door, the cops shot him.

As soon as I'd read the article, I called my mother. "Have you seen the front page of the *World-Herald* yet?" I asked. Even though my parents lived 170 miles from Omaha, they were also subscribers to Nebraska's one major newspaper.

"No. Why?"

I wanted her to be surprised when she saw the full-color photo. A lone police officer stood in the center of Izard Street, but in the foreground the rear end of Dad's red truck appeared parked curbside behind the yellow slash of police tape. The truck's cameo in the news was evidence proving my proximity to, what I considered, an extraordinary occurrence. It was violence, plain and simple, but it was somehow an exciting jolt out of routine, too.

"Isn't that incredible? Dad's old Mazda made the front page," I blurted as soon as she'd seen the picture.

"What if you'd been in the truck?" she asked.

"But I wasn't."

While it wasn't hard for me to imagine being raped, it was much harder to imagine being shot. A few days later, when I got the truck out of impound and examined the bullet holes for myself, a sort of dumbstruck awe came over me. There were three bullet holes: one in the metal frame of the driver's side door, one that pierced through the seatbelt as it hung slack behind the seat, and one, on the passenger side, as the bullet exited. Knowing nothing about how bullets can ricochet, I reassured myself: *even if you'd been in the truck the bullet wouldn't have hit you.* I also took pride in the fact that the Omaha PD had done such a good job by protecting me from a violent criminal.

After the shooting, I went on living on Izard Street without fear. Even the reminder of the bullet holes vanished when I returned the borrowed truck to my dad. I forgot all about the shooting until fifteen years later when the defense attorney asked if I'd ever been a victim of violent crime. And now I knew the real answer. If I'd really been a victim, I'd have experienced some harm or injury that day. I wouldn't have felt the strange excitement, nor would I have taken such comfort in being protected by the police. How had I so quickly dismissed what happened? I doubt my placid obliviousness was the result of being high—if anything that would have made me more paranoid about my surroundings, nor was it just the invincibility of my youth. I believed I'd always be safe from gun violence because doing so made me feel less vulnerable. Along with this self-absorption came the inability to empathize. At the time it never occurred to me that Jay's proximity to this violence put him more danger than me. I never asked, "What if—just because of his location and the color of his skin—the cops had mistaken Jay for Greenlow?"

Jay and I never talked about how he felt when Mr. MGM treated him as if he were dangerous. We never talked about the shooting or how we felt in the aftermath. We never talked about the circumstances that made us afraid. We had inherited powerlessness: Jay because he was Black, me because I was a woman. Jay never mentioned fearing cops. I never talked about how I almost got raped. It seemed too painful and too shameful to mention. We coped by getting high and by taking our raw tenderness and expressing it sexually. I must have been attracted to Jay's gentleness, how he always made sure that I was comfortable with whatever we did in bed. He sought my consent and having the power to say what I wanted or didn't helped me heal after being sexually assaulted.

What would have happened if Jay and I tried out a future together? Sometimes at work that summer, I'd see mixed race couples eating with their children, beautiful babies with almond-mocha skin, wildly curly hair, and shocking blue eyes. If Jay and I had kids, I thought, they'd look like that. Much

WHAT WILL OUTLAST ME?

later, I'd see this as a pattern I have with men—to imagine a future that suited me, without taking into account my partner's feelings or desires. At the time I thought I loved Jay, but love is the wrong word to describe what we had. It was something more akin to expediency. I greedily soaked up what I wanted from him, whether it was protection, high-quality pot, or sexual pleasure. I never stopped to think about what he needed, and in this I was a lot like my old roommates' cocky friends who saw lovers not as equals but as sexual conquests.

By that fall, once school started again, Jay and I had begun to drift apart. I cut back my hours at Chili's and stopped smoking so much pot so I could focus on my schoolwork, which meant I started to see less of Jay. The day after 9/11 we went to Olive Garden for dinner, and all Jay wanted to talk about were the World Trade Center attacks. I stuffed myself with breadsticks while he asked me questions about what had happened. Will terrorists strike Omaha because we have an Air Force base here? How many people do you think were killed? Will we run out of oil now? Is there going to be a war? His incessant questions—and my inability to give him answers—made me uncomfortable. Now it seems strange to me that the Twin Towers falling upset him more than the shooting. But 9/11 was different than the shooting. It made us collectively, as Americans, all vulnerable. His constant string of questions made him seem childlike. As I sat across the booth from him, shoving stray parmesan crumbs across the table with my fingertip, I knew our relationship was doomed. Now instead of being tender, he was just vulnerable, and incapable of protecting me.

The feeling of safety he'd given me dissolved, and with it went our brief romance. I broke up with him a week later.

After Jay and I broke up, my father told me, "I knew you'd come to your senses. There was no use telling you why you shouldn't date a Black man. I thought you'd figure it out on your own, and you did."

"What is that supposed to mean?" I demanded.

"Well, you know."

"No, I don't."

"It would have made things harder for you."

I tried to explain to my father that he knew nothing about the reasons why I dumped Jay. He didn't know that my relationship with Jay revolved around our partying, or how his proximity as a co-worker made it an easy relationship to fall into. Yet something still nagged at me. Once I'd used up the easy comfort my relationship with Jay afforded me, I discarded him. My father saw the racial divide as a line that shouldn't be crossed, but it wasn't because of who Jay was as an individual, it was because of his context in the world. Because Jay was Black, he was vulnerable. This was the system of the culture we lived in. Even though I thought that I made these choices independently and of my own volition, a big factor influencing me was the power structure, which until now, had been nearly invisible.

*

Shortly after I was dismissed from serving on the jury in Georgia, I took a summer job teaching reading to kindergarteners. The job required travelling to Alabama. Early

WHAT WILL OUTLAST ME?

one evening as I was checking into my hotel, a news alert about George Zimmerman blared from the TV over the front desk. Zimmerman had been on trial for shooting Trayvon Martin, an unarmed black teenager. It announced his acquittal based on the ruling that he had acted in self-defense.

"I can't believe they let him off," I said, as I handed my company credit card over. I had been following the trial and believed that as a violent, gun-toting man, Zimmerman was clearly guilty.

"I know," said the hotel clerk. The newscast showed footage taken at the scene of the shooting: Trayvon Martin's body, dead on the ground, just the way I remembered seeing Greenlow's body. Though I knew that the circumstances leading up to these two shootings were different, in the end, they were eerily similar. It wasn't just the lasting images that stuck with me: the dark, baggie jeans, the sprawled limbs, but the fact that Zimmerman's jury believed he had been threatened to the point of needing to defend himself. Many evil deeds are falsely justified by fear.

When I got to my room, I took my laptop out and set it up on the ugly laminate desk. Now that the shooting on Izard Street was on my mind, I wondered what had become of Jay. I started searching for him, first on Facebook and then in broader Google searches. He has a common surname, which made him virtually incognito. I kept searching, but nothing came up. I wondered what I would message him if his Facebook profile popped up. Maybe I could start with this: I'm sorry I was so selfish. I know it's not a good excuse, but I was afraid.

KILLING CHICKENS

Dad is going to kill Scrambly because I asked him to. I hold her tucked under my arm like a football. "You've been a good chicken," I tell her. "Thanks for all the eggs." Her breed, Golden Comet, is known for good egg production. She cocks her reptilian eye at me and clucks, a low cooing sound. I stroke her bright-red comb, always surprisingly hot to the touch. Though her scaly feet are caked with chicken manure, her reddish-brown feathers still have that pleasant, dusty smell they had when she was a three-day old chick under a heat lamp.

"I'm sorry," I whisper.

Dad is visiting me from Nebraska. I live in Bowling Green, Ohio, a town of 30,000 people, known for its state university—where my husband is finishing his PhD—and for its National Tractor Pull, the largest annual tractor pulling competition in the country. Dad's here for the tractor pull. When I asked him if he'd help me butcher my chickens during his visit, he scoffed.

"You can't do it yourself?"

I had learned to butcher chickens with my mom and Aunt Beth when we lived on the farm before I learned how to read.

"Those chickens didn't have names," I said.

WHAT WILL OUTLAST ME?

Dad was a bad father, but he was good with animals. He preg-checked heifers, bottle-fed orphaned calves, rescued mourning doves from grain bins, dug worms for ducks, and castrated hogs. He was good at killing, too. When my sister's dog, Cookie, surprised a porcupine and got a face full of quills, rather than pay for vet bills we couldn't afford, Dad shot the dog. He wasn't abusive, just neglectful. Mom took up the slack, so I came out okay. She didn't divorce Dad until I went to college. Still, I felt like a single-parent child. Dad never attended my cheerleading or 4-H competitions, never went to parent-teacher conferences. If he couldn't drink at an event, he wouldn't go.

Augusts in Bowling Green are hot and sticky. Cicadas screech in the elm trees. My husband and I rent a bungalow a few blocks from campus. For the past three years, I've kept three laying hens in the backyard to cure me of a bout of depression that this place inspired.

My days here are numbered now. In a few months, my husband, Kent, will graduate, then we'll move to Georgia, where he found a post-doc lecturer position. The chickens have gotten old. In their prime they each laid an egg a day. Now I'm lucky to get an egg out of them every two weeks. My hobby-farmer friend Candy said, "If they're not laying, they're just feed burners." She declined requests to butcher them for me and suggested I take them to a small slaughterhouse. The only one that would do the job was a six-hour round trip drive from where I lived and expensive.

I didn't feel up to doing it myself. I knew chickens weren't really pets, but I'd treated these hens as though they were.

SARAH K. LENZ

Scrambly, Franny, and Zooey were tame as housecats. They didn't mind being picked up and petted. I saved choice kale trimmings and apple cores for them. When the cicadas molted, I gathered the shells that clung to the elm tree's bark, treats that my chickens gobbled. They gave me a comforting morning routine. I'd make my coffee, then go—cup in hand—out to the coop to feed them. In the calm morning, they greeted me with clucks and still-warm eggs.

If not for the National Tractor Pull, my dad would never have come here. He hates to travel. Since I left Nebraska for grad school six years ago, he hadn't visited once. In the mid-70s, before I was born, he was a puller. He kept boxes of pulling trophies tucked away in the closet of Mom's sewing room. I used to play with them, polishing the shiny gold trophy tractors, lining them up according to size. The largest—for the Grand Champion Pull-Off—stood close to four feet tall.

Dad had a few years' success with pulling—winning the Sherman County Fair Pull, the Fall Festival Pull, and a dozen others. Then the National Tractor Puller's Association changed the rules. Before, tractors were judged on the percentage of their own weight they pulled, so Dad's small, modified Farmall was hard to beat. When the association did away with percentage pulls—tractors won by pulling the most weight no matter how much they weighed—bigger was better—so Dad built a bigger tractor in 1981, the year I was born. I suffered from colic. My cries permeated every room in the house. It was January, the slow time for farmers. Aside from checking on his feeder cattle once a day, my father had no work.

WHAT WILL OUTLAST ME?

"I spent that whole winter out in the shop, building that tractor," he told me. "I did it mostly to get away from your screaming."

Mom's version is different: "He liked staying out in the shop because he thought he could hide his drinking that way." Years after my mom divorced him, she told me, "Rolly's been an alcoholic as long as I've known him."

Dad named his new tractor Rolly's Folly. His mother-in-law, my Grandma Betty, suggested the name. She'd always thought my dad's endeavors foolish. He went with it, thinking the rhyme was clever. Drunk on his inaugural run, he knocked over the gasoline pump next to the farm garage. Mom kept a photo of it; she wanted to hold him accountable, I guess, or she wanted to document how close he came to an explosion. Over the years, though, it's been less a cautionary tale and more a family joke.

I was born too late to know Dad's triumphs. Like thousands of farmers, Dad lost his farm during the market crash of the '80s. When he was still happily farming, he painted Folly red, lettering her name across the chassis, but he never won a single pull with that tractor. He sold Folly almost 30 years ago, but he still loves watching tractor pulling.

*

When I picked him up from the airport two days ago, I was surprised by how withered he looked. He's always been tall—six foot four—tan and muscular from outdoor manual labor, but now, at 60, his wrinkled, weather-beaten skin hangs from his bones, and he looks more hunched than I remembered. He comes off the plane a bit bewildered and shaky. His only luggage is a small carry-on duffle bag emblazed with the

Marlboro logo, which he redeemed after collecting hundreds of Marlboro-mile stamps. As soon as the airport terminal's automatic sliding doors shut behind us, Dad lights up a smoke. I wait because I don't want him to smoke in my car. Little did I know, my request wouldn't make a difference. He complains about how much he hates flying, as if he does it all the time, even though this is the first time he's been on a plane in decades. He finishes his first cigarette and lights a second. Halfway through this one, color seeps back into his cheeks.

Three days from now, on the last day of Dad's visit, we plan to butcher the chickens. The National Tractor Pull runs Friday through Sunday. Each day, there are two sessions starting at noon and 7 p.m. Dad wants to attend it all, which means 36 hours.

"I just don't get it," my friend James says. "What's so fun about a bunch of Republican rednecks watching obnoxious exhaust-spewing tractors?"

I think about how after sitting in the stands at a tractor pull, my face will be gritty with dirt from the track and how, if I forget to bring ear plugs, my ears will ring all the next day, and how the patriotism and God-Bless-'Merica spirit at these events is propagandistic and misogynistic. I have trouble explaining the allure. For me, being a child had meant going to a lot of tractor pulls and showing appropriate awe when Dad fired up Folly. If he wanted to take me for a ride after drinking a twelve-pack, I didn't dare say no—even if it terrified me when he opened the throttle, hitting 80 miles an hour on country gravel roads. I sat on his lap in the open cab, bugs hitting my face, the roar of the engine so loud it rattled my sternum.

WHAT WILL OUTLAST ME?

On the first day of the tractor pull, I drop Dad off at the front gate to the Wood County fairgrounds. I spend the afternoon in my garden. Even miles from the fairgrounds, I hear the tractors rev, their mechanical grunting echoing across town. Tayveon, my five-year-old neighbor, helps me in the garden. He comes out to play when he sees me working. We collect slugs from under the cucumbers and feed them to the chickens. He squeals in delight when he sees the chickens fight over a particularly large slug. We pick tomatoes and peppers to give to Tayveon's mom, Shanika. She's a single mom, and she often checks with me to make sure Tayveon isn't over-wearing his welcome. I always tell her I like his company. I've been worried about how Tayveon will take the chicken butchering. He's become attached to them, but I remember I was his age when I first watched my mom kill chickens. Back then I felt more curiosity than anything else. After gutting one chicken, Mom showed me its purple gizzard, cutting it open revealing the gravel-filled crop. "Chickens don't have teeth, so this is how they chew," she said, and I thought that was cool.

When Shanika calls Tayveon to come in, I meet her at her front door and give her the vegetables. Once Tayveon is out of earshot I explain that Dad and I are going to butcher the chickens.

"Don't tell Tayveon you're going to kill them. He tells the kids at school about them," she says.

"Maybe you should keep him out of the yard Sunday afternoon."

She agrees. "I'll tell him they went to go live on a farm."

When I pick Dad up after the first tractor pull session, he's equally elated and pissed. He's upset about the concessions.

"Can you believe they don't sell beer? What kind of dopes made that rule?"

From the passenger seat, he lights a cigarette, and explains that beer isn't sold within the fairground gates, but spectators can bring their own, as long as it's in a cooler no longer than 12 inches. He's annoyed that he didn't know this before I dropped him off miles from the nearest package store.

I take him to Walmart. He buys two cases of Old Milwaukee, three small coolers, and three beer koozies printed with American flags. I buy foam ear plugs and sunscreen. As soon as we get home from the store, Dad installs himself on the back patio, where he can watch the chickens graze, drink beer, and chain smoke until the evening tractor pull starts. He's impressed by the chickens' set up.

"Go get yourself a beer," he says.

I don't want one, but I don't know what else to do with him, so I grab a can and slip a koozie on it.

"That's pretty neat, the way you made their coop," he says when I return.

I built the coop with a salvaged rabbit hutch I found on Craigslist. I enclosed the rabbit cages with plywood to make them winter-tight and added a nesting box and roosts. I constructed a pen with chicken wire and scrap lumber pulled from Candy's junk pile. The whole project cost twenty dollars. Dad's noticeably proud of my thrift and inventiveness. "I built Folly with junkyard parts," he reminds me.

WHAT WILL OUTLAST ME?

Now that he's drained three cans of beer, he's more talkative. He tells me about building Folly, starting with a differential—a simple gear train and axles—he found at Grint Salvage Yard. "I told 'em I'd paint their name on the tractor if they'd give me the parts, and they did." Gradually he accumulated enough parts to weld a tractor together, and once built, he kept rebuilding it for years. When the first engine wore down, he talked Uncle Corwin into giving him a Ford 440 from one of his junker cars. When the torque from pulling so much weight broke the hub bolts connecting the tires to the axles, he explains how he sweet-talked Grandpa Harvey into letting him take the hubs off the old farm tractor.

He gets melancholy, as I've seen often when he drinks. "I never won any pulls because I couldn't afford good tires. People started pouring serious money their tractors, and then I didn't stand a chance."

I take a sip of beer. Franny scratches in the grass, looking for grubs. Zooey ruffles her feathers and preens. Their soft clucking reminds me of whispered confessions.

"Then the farm went to shit. I pulled until Folly sold on the foreclosure auction." He belches a beer-gut rumbler, then brightens— "I forgot how chickens cluck like that. Boy, that sure brings back memories."

Saturday night, Kent and I go to the tractor pull with Dad. Before we leave, he stuffs a six-pack in a cooler for each of us. The coolers are bright red and zippered, like school lunchboxes, and I feel like a child again, going along with whatever Dad wants. Kent and I will drink only a few beers, and Dad will down the rest until he slurs and stumbles, but we will pretend that nothing is wrong.

We pay twenty dollars each for tickets. There are easily 400 people in attendance. Concession booths line the backside of the grandstands where one can buy funnel cake and deep-fried Oreos, BBQ and burgers, cotton candy and lemonade. Dad chooses prime seats in the bleachers.

This is Kent's first tractor pull, so we explain that the object is to pull a weighted sled the farthest down a 300-foot-long dirt track. The sleds are shaped like the Lego creations Kent builds as a hobby, but the cab where the sled operator sits reminds me of a giant praying mantis head. The weights slide on a complex system of hydraulics so that 35,000 pounds slide from the rear axle of the sled forward, which makes the pulling harder the farther the tractor pulls. If a tractor pulls the entire 300 feet without stopping, the crowd erupts, screaming FULL PULL.

Tonight, the Unlimited Modified Tractors compete, the largest and loudest. These machines have names like Rock Hard Ram, Silver Bullet, and Mr. Mac Daddy, and are often built with six or eight engines fused together on an elongated chassis. They don't have mufflers. When they run, black billows of smoke pour from their header pipes. Sometimes engines catch fire and pit crews race toward the flaming tractors with fire extinguishers. The crowd loves that.

After a dozen runs, I'm bored by how all the tractors look the same, so I people watch. Women wear Daisy Dukes so short their ass-cheeks hang out. They flash midriffs by knotting their T-shirts. "Tractor Pullers Do It in the Dirt," I read, lettered across one women's chest.

WHAT WILL OUTLAST ME?

Two young men sit in the bleachers in front of us. Between the tractor roars, Dad strikes up a conversation with them. They both wear Wrangler jeans. One wears a cap with the Snap-On tool logo, the other, a brand of GMO seed corn. Like Dad, they clip pliers to their belts, and, like him, these are the type of men who know how to fix broken engines.

As Dad starts telling them about Folly, his face lights up. One man tells my dad that he builds pivot irrigation systems for a living. They talk about engines in a technical way that shuts Kent and me out of the conversation, so Kent leaves to buy concessions. They speculate about which tractor will win this division based on criteria I don't understand. It's obvious my dad charms them. They insist he drink a Keystone Light they pull from their cooler.

The next day, Kent tells me he feels sad and squeamish about killing the chickens and doesn't want to be home when we do it between the day's tractor-pulling sessions, so he spends the afternoon at Starbucks. I'd join him if I could. When I was a child, butchering chickens was women's work. My mom slit their throats with efficiency and nonchalance. Blood squirted from their jugulars and sprayed the dirt and mallow weeds in the chicken yard. The chickens squawked raggedly, and their wings flapped violently for longer than seemed possible after losing so much blood. Squirted with layers of blood, my mother's old tennis shoes looked like a Jackson Pollock painting.

"You should kill them behind the spiraea," I tell Dad. Though I'm hungover from last night's beer-drinking, he seems in fine fettle, even after he left his dinner—a hamburger from a concession stand wrapped in foil—untouched on my kitchen table. The chickens hadn't eaten either. That morning, I let the chickens out of the coop, but didn't give them breakfast, so gutting wouldn't be as messy. I checked the nesting box for eggs, empty. For the fifth day in a row. This made me feel better. I tell myself: *They're old chickens. I gave them a good life.*

My chickens spent happy hours dustbathing under the spiraea, and along with the worm-filled compost pile, it was one of their favorite places in the yard. The spiraea also offered privacy. It'll shield Dad from Tayveon's house next door, and if I stand around the corner of the house, I won't have to look either. I feel sick to my stomach from worrying about my dad's drinking and from too many chili cheese fries washed down with beer at the tractor pull. Maybe what's sloshing in my gut is regret and guilt. I wish I didn't have to kill my chickens, and I feel guilty for making him do the dirty work. I don't want his help, but I'm desperate.

"I can't watch," I say. I thought he'd make fun of me, or call me a wuss, but he doesn't. Before I hand over Scrambly, he decides to kneel down on the grass. He grunts as he lowers to the ground. He's unsteady, catching himself with a hand plant. I hope he can hold the butcher knife without shaking.

While Dad slits Scrambly's throat, I grab Zooey from the pen next. I tell her "Thank you," hoping she can feel my gratitude. I want her to have a quick death, a good death.

"Are you done?" I ask.

From around the corner of the house, he calls back: "Almost."

WHAT WILL OUTLAST ME?

I peek. He's holding Scrambly down with both hands so she won't thrash. Her blood seeps through the grass, into the ground. When she's finally still, we repeat the ritual until all three chickens are dead.

I carry the dead birds by their feet to the back patio where I prepared a five-gallon bucket of scalding water. Their eyelids have glazed over with a white membrane, reminding me of cartoons with X-ed out eyes. In death, their fawn-brown feathers have lost their smoothness and ruffle in the breeze.

The first step in butchering is dipping the carcasses into boiling water to loosen their feathers. We don't talk much as we work. We want to get this over as quickly as possible. I plunge Scrambly's body into the bucket and let the steaming water roll off her. A scalded chicken's feathers smell like wet dog mixed with rust. When I grab the feathers and pull, they make a ripping sound like tangled hair being torn from hairbrush bristles. Once all three are plucked, I feel better because without feathers they are as indistinguishable and anonymous as rubber gag chickens. Unlike plump grocery-store chickens, my old birds are scrawny. Their breast bones jut out in sharp ridges. I pick out every stray pin feather. Then I take Dad's Bic and singe stray hairs off their pimpled skin.

"Look how yellow their skin is," Dad says. "That's a sign they ate good. Lots of corn."

That's when I notice the gashed wounds on their necks. One neck looks like it was dully—and painfully—sawed at. *Wasn't the butcher knife sharp enough? Was my father inept? Could I have done better?* I try to shake these thoughts. Some things can't be changed. Dad cuts off their heads and feet and throws them in the gut bucket with the feathers.

SARAH K. LENZ

We take the birds into the kitchen to gut them because we need a sink for rinsing. I'm unsure of making the right cuts, so Dad does this part, slitting them open like envelopes at the cloaca. Then working from the other end, he slices the windpipe and esophagus free from the neck, scooping out the guts in one swift movement. They release with a sucking sound. I get a whiff of ammonia from shit-filled intestines, earthy and metallic. He hands me the carcass for a final rinse and begins sorting through the guts. I stick my hand inside the still-warm cavity and use my fingers to scrape out the red lung attached to the rib cage. It shreds like a sponge. I rinse the body well and seal it in a freezer bag.

"What do you want to keep?" he asks.

"Save the livers. I'll fry them for supper."

"Want the heart?" He holds up a small piece knotted with clots of fat. It doesn't look like any heart I've ever seen.

"Are you sure that's the heart?"

"Oh," he says. He squints, holding it up to the light. "It's an asshole."

The knotted, rubbery bit was the cloaca made muscular from so much egg laying. He tosses it into the gut bucket, embarrassed.

"I need a smoke," he says. He washes his hands and leaves me to finish the job. I think about what it means to confuse a heart and an asshole.

I cut the gallbladders from the edible livers and leave them to soak in a dish of milk. As I'm scooping up the last of the guts to throw away, I feel something hard. It's an unlaid egg, sheathed in the oviduct. Then I see the rest of them—dozens of unformed eggs sprouting from the ovaries. The developing yolks are like miniature suns or clusters of deep orange pearls.

She had more eggs to give me, I think. *I gave up on her.*

After the birds are tucked into the freezer, I clean the sink and counters with bleach. I grab the unlaid egg and two beers from the fridge and join Dad on the back patio. He's hosed the chicken blood off the cement and dumped the feathers and guts in the garbage. A few lazy horseflies hover above the still-wet cement. When we sit down at the patio table, I hand Dad his beer. I set the egg on the table.

"Look what I found inside one of the chickens."

"I'll be damned," he says.

We watch as the egg wobbles on the glass patio table for a moment. Then it stops, reaching an equilibrium. I pop open my can and take a big swig. The cold beer tastes good. I'm grateful Dad helped me, and I feel spent. Dad looks tired, too. We hear the first tractor rev from the fairgrounds.

"We should get going. You're going to miss it."

"Naw, that's okay," he says. "It's nice to be here."

He lights a cigarette and takes another drink of beer. And then he takes another.

MAKING HEADCHEESE

A whole hog's head soaks in my kitchen sink, bobbing on its side. Rivulets of blood melt into the cold water. The head is partially skinned. Long, feminine lashes rim its blue-gray eyes. Snout and lips are turned up in a slight sneer, revealing rather human-looking incisors.

It's ten o'clock. Kent is already at work for his lunch shift at The Milky Way Restaurant in downtown Boise where he is a server. I waited for him to leave before taking the head—which had been butchered the day before—out of the refrigerator. I'm going to make headcheese with it. Kent had made it clear he thinks the endeavor grotesque.

The hog's glassy eye stares at me and my stomach flutters with nausea. I begin to think this project was a terrible mistake. The idea had bloomed suddenly after I read *How to Cook a Wolf*, M.F.K. Fischer's 1942 book about coping with wartime food shortages. She explains how her Aunt Gwen used to make "cold shape." From what I'd been told, cold shape was identical to my Grandma Lillian's headcheese except it called for a calves' head rather than a pig's head. Headcheese is made from the boiled scraps of cheeks, ears, snout, and tongue suspended in a gelatin made from the head's cartilage and served cold, essentially a chunky meat Jell-O.

WHAT WILL OUTLAST ME?

Making headcheese was the most recent in a long string of projects inspired by books. As soon as I learned to read, I spent hours poring over the Childcraft Encyclopedia volume entitled *Make & Do*. For the mid-eighties, its pages were nostalgically out of date. Children pictured looked wholesome, earthy, and quaint in Afros and bellbottoms. Projects were homey and resourceful: salt-dough sculpting clay, Popsicle stick houses, fingerpainting, and macramé. During lonely afternoons on the farm, I entertained myself for hours with that book. Perhaps this urge to plunge into ambitious projects was something inherited. My Grandma Krahulik had always been one to make and do. She upcycled long before the term was coined. She made beautiful, shaggy rugs from bright scraps of polyester fabric. She mounted broken costume jewelry bought at garage sales on black velvet to depict peacocks or Christmas trees. She also was the only person I'd ever known to make headcheese.

Loneliness might have also triggered this project. Lately I'd found myself thinking a lot about Grandma Lillian, who'd been dead for twelve years. I was in my second year of grad school in Idaho, and all my family, including my parents—who'd just suffered a divorce—were a thousand miles away in Nebraska. I thought maybe making headcheese would somehow connect me to my heritage.

My first memory of headcheese was from when I was six years old and had walked into Grandma Lillian's kitchen to find her facing off with a decapitated pig's head, as if worshipping the Lord of the Flies himself. It had floppy puppy-like ears. Its marble eyes stared at me above a gaping mouth from which a lolling, insolent tongue waggled off to the side. After that I'd never even ventured a single bite of headcheese.

SARAH K. LENZ

Now at twenty-six, I'd had a few culinary adventures: the thrilling first time I let a raw oyster slide down my throat, or the time I worked up the courage to try fried beef testicles and found them delicious. In the early 2000s, the nose-to-tail food movement was just starting, so I'd dipped cautiously into cooking with organ meats by making liver pâtés. Fischer's food writing played a part, too. Her description of cold shape captivated me. The head's eye had a "savory wink" and the "lone ear lopped loose and faintly pink" next to "the odd wrinkles of the forehead." She believed that those who eat such delicacies have "a God-given and intelligently self-cultivated sense of gastronomical freedom." Part of me wanted to feel sophisticated and brave. At the time, the irony of making such a homely dish as headcheese to feel worldly and liberated, was lost on me.

Headcheese is technically offal. Derived from Germanic roots, the word offal means "garbage" or literally "off-fall," the unwanted scraps that fall off the butcher's table. Maybe the only reason Grandma Lillian had made headcheese was because of her thrift. She never threw anything away that still had usefulness. Swarms of rubber bands from the daily newspaper infested her kitchen drawers. She saved up table scraps in paper milk cartons with the tops splayed open for us to take home to our dog.

Grandma would be proud that I had procured this head for free, I thought.

A few weeks ago, when I first had the notion to make headcheese, I told my friend Andrea, who was a chef. She got

WHAT WILL OUTLAST ME?

excited because she used to make it when she worked charcuterie for Wolfgang Puck.

"I'll teach you," she said while we sat in her cluttered office. I'd just eaten a dozen Kumamoto oysters on the half shell in her restaurant, The Milky Way (where Kent worked), and had stopped by her office above the dining room to say hi. She pointed out the logical next step, too: "You'll have to find a fresh head. Otherwise it's not worth it."

Because none of the butchers, restaurant wholesalers, or grocery stores in Boise could procure heads, I put an ad on Craigslist: "Wanted Fresh Hog's Head." Within twenty-four hours, I had two nibbles. The first guy wanted $10, the other, a man named Tony told me I could have it for free since he planned to throw it away. He'd scheduled hog butchering for the following weekend.

*

My urge to make headcheese was driven in part by wistfulness. Over the decade since Grandma Lillian had passed away, I had heard stories about her teaching my mother to make headcheese when she was my age—in her twenties—and newly married. I'd also heard how good it was. I called my mom back in Nebraska for more details.

"But what does it taste like?" I asked.

"I don't know how to explain. It's just pork. It's very good."

I was hoping she could give me some guidance or at least a recipe, but it turned out she couldn't remember how they had made it.

"Can't you just find a recipe on the internet?" she asked.

In addition to consulting Fischer's recipe, I had already researched recipes online. They included instructions like, *Thoroughly brush the teeth and tongue*, and *Use a disposable razor to shave the hog's facial hair. Singe off any remaining hair with a blow torch.*

"I've looked at some recipes, but I want to know exactly how you and Grandma used to make it. That's what I want to recreate."

"You don't have a pressure canner, do you?"

"No. Why?"

"Well, that's how we used to do it."

When she said that I remembered Dad sitting at Grandma's kitchen table, spooning globs of gelatinous pork broth dappled with meat chunks out of a quart Mason jar. The headcheese made a sucking sound as it released from the glass jar. I decided then that canning it was out.

Though my parents rarely agreed on anything after their divorce, they did still share a reverence for headcheese. When I called my dad, he expressed his love for the dish too, though he ridiculed Mom's side of the family because they wouldn't eat headcheese. "Grandpa B wouldn't even try headcheese. He used to say, 'You put them eyeballs in there? Are they delicious?'"

"Well, are they?" I asked.

"No. You don't put the eyeballs in. That's ridiculous."

I realized then that I had no idea what I was doing trying to cook a whole hog's head.

*

When I'd spoken with Tony from Craigslist, he invited me to come watch the butchering. I accepted with a curious mix of

WHAT WILL OUTLAST ME?

excitement and trepidation. I called my mom back to tell her I was going to see the slaughter.

"When we slaughtered hogs on the farm, I was the blood catcher," she said and explained how they had mixed pig's blood with oatmeal to make sausage. This was something else I'd missed out on. The family farm had dwindled to financial ruin and was foreclosed on by the time I reached second grade. I tried to picture my mother kneeling in front of a hog, a bowl between her knees sloshing with ruby-colored blood, but it was hard for me to imagine her overcoming disgust to impress her mother-in-law. Now that my parents were divorced, it was easier to remember how much friction there had been between Mom and my paternal grandparents. Mom threw away the Christmas presents Grandma gave me.

"They're dirty old things from yard sales," she said, dumping a tea set ringed with lipstick stains into the trash pail. Mom had also never liked eating at her in-laws' house and whenever we were asked to stay for dinner, made excuses: "We had a late lunch," she'd say, or "I already have dinner in the crockpot." This infuriated my father, but I sided with Mom. By the time I was old enough to remember meals at Grandma and Grandpa Krahulik's, Grandpa had taken over the cooking because of the accident. His meals were greasy, grisly, and gray. The leftovers he reheated bore no resemblance to the goulash or pork chop he'd started with. On the rare occasions when we ate there, I spread the food across my worn melamine plate and held my breath to avoid tasting the few forkfuls that entered my mouth. My mother did the same.

After the accident, Grandma only cooked for special occasions and had only two dishes in her repertoire: headcheese and *kolache*—a Czechoslovakian pastry, similar to a Danish, filled with fruit or poppy seeds. The only thing I ever enjoyed eating at Grandma's were her cherry *kolache*. But even then, my mom reminded me her pastries weren't as good as they used to be. "Before the accident, she made the dough from scratch," Mom explained. "Now she uses frozen bread dough. It's just not the same." Nor was Grandma, apparently. "Too bad you didn't know your grandma before the accident," I'd often heard my parents say.

I was four years old when it happened, too little to remember. According to my father, Grandpa had been driving their green Oldsmobile when he fell asleep. Grandma slept in the passenger's seat beside him and had taken off her seatbelt to be more comfortable. When their car collided with another head-on, Grandpa walked away from the accident with minor scrapes, but Grandma was thrown head-first into the dashboard.

"You should have seen it," Dad told me. "Her head left a dent twelve inches deep." Miraculously she survived, but her memory and personality were always just a bit off after the accident.

*

The next Saturday morning I arrived at Tony's. He didn't live on a farm as I'd imagined, but in a modern ranch-style house on a two-acre lot just off the interstate. I arrived in time to see Tony, dressed in jeans and a blue flannel shirt (and looking uncannily like Bob Vila), walking across the yard with a shotgun held in his clenched hands.

WHAT WILL OUTLAST ME?

I followed him across the dirt yard, past a two-car garage, and toward a livestock pen. Before I saw where he aimed, I heard the shot. Over the side of the fence, I saw the pig. It staggered gently to the ground, head wobbling. With a butcher knife Tony sliced into the pig's throat, hitting the main artery. Blood gushed with each pulse of the pig's dying heart like waves lapping the edge of a lake. Standing a safe distance from the action, I couldn't take my eyes off the brilliant gush of blood. The hog didn't make a sound.

Tony and his friend, Vern, pierced a meat hook through the hog's rear ankles and hoisted the carcass by pulley to a manageable level where it dangled from a fifteen-foot tall wooden tripod. They peeled the black and white hide off, inside out, like removing long underwear. The pig hung naked, save for a mohawk-like strip of black wiry hairs along its forehead.

Working in tandem, Vern and Tony sliced open the chest cavity for gutting. I held my breath, waiting for horror-movie gore, but sighed when I saw the immaculate beauty of the entrails. Sealed in their own membranes, each organ was discreet: purple-veined water balloon of bladder, gray rope coils of intestine, burgundy-jewel slab of liver. The meat smelled clean and fresh.

Vern kneeled on the ground in his camouflage fatigues, but he looked more MacGyver than soldier. He started to cut off the head by making an incision through the neck muscles. It wiggled like a bobblehead doll. The tricky part was slicing through the spine. Due to the curvature of each vertebra, it was impossible to make a straight cut. Vern worked the knife, jiggling it at different angles. With a cracking sound, the spine severed. Tony caught the head before it hit the ground. He hosed it down and chunks of god-knows-what flew out of the mouth.

"We'll get this packed up for you," Tony said, as he put the head in a garbage bag. I felt like I should be doing something to help him, but I didn't know what. He twisted the neck of the garbage bag shut and handed it to me. The weight of it startled me. Easily twenty pounds of flesh and bone, it felt like I carried a giant bowling ball. I put it in my Geo Metro hatchback and thanked Tony.

On the drive home, the head seeped blood, which pooled in the bottom of the bag. When I removed it from the car, I dripped a trail of blood up the front sidewalk to my house. I left the head on the stoop and went to get more garbage bags to reinforce the leaky one. At Tony's I hadn't touched any pig parts, and I was still too squeamish to take the head out of its bag with my bare hands. With the head re-shrouded in plastic and put in a 9"-by-13" baking pan to catch any more leaks, I carried it into the kitchen. Kent saw the hog's snout poking up from behind its plastic shroud.

"What are you doing with that?" he asked, even though he knew about my plans to make headcheese with Andrea the next day.

"I'm putting it in the fridge."

"With the rest of our food?"

"Where else?"

"I don't know. It's gross, Hon." He eyed the deep indentations the hog's nostrils made in the plastic while I rummaged around in the fridge until I cleared a space on the bottom shelf.

WHAT WILL OUTLAST ME?

"Just don't look in there if it bothers you that much," I said. I was annoyed he was acting so squeamish about it because I wanted some sort of reassurance I could handle this. I didn't like that I was just a repulsed as he was, and I didn't want to admit it.

*

The next morning after Kent left for work, I worked up the courage to remove the head from the fridge. Tony told me I needed to soak the head in cold water to draw the blood out. My stomach clinched when I caught a whiff of the blood with its dull iron aroma. I rolled the head out of the garbage bag and into the sink without touching it. I took a deep breath—AH—and pressed a finger into the skinned cheek. It felt no different than a rump roast. I remembered what Fischer wrote: "Why is it worse, in the end, to see an animal's head cooked and prepared for our pleasure than a thigh or a rib?" I'd managed to overcome one hurdle of revulsion.

An hour later in Andrea's kitchen, I unwrapped the soaked head. Even in her home kitchen, she worked with the efficient energy of a professional chef. Without flinching she carved out the eyeballs with a flick of her filet knife around the eye socket. When the eye came out, the eyelashes were still attached. They looked human. Then Andrea scalped the hog's mohawk with startling swiftness.

After another thorough scrubbing of the mouth, teeth, and tongue, we put the head in an industrial sized pot Andrea had borrowed from The Milky Way's kitchen. We added carrots, onions, bay leaves, bunches of fresh parsley and sage, peppercorns, cloves, and a bottle of white wine. We covered everything with water and set it to simmer for eight hours.

SARAH K. LENZ

While we were waiting, Andrea said, "There's something I want to show you." She handed me her mint-condition, first edition of Fischer's *The Art of Eating*. I turned to the passage about offal and read: "When you eat a stuffed baked bull's heart, or a grilled lamb's brain or a 'mountain oyster,' you need not choke them down with nauseated resolve to be braver or wiser or more potent, but with plain delight."

"Headcheese isn't for everyone," Andrea tried to reassure me. "It's okay if you don't like it."

I had been so caught up with the logistics of the project and repulsed by the decapitated head itself that I hadn't really thought about how when it was all done, and how even if I had the courage to eat it, I still might find headcheese unpalatable. At first it had felt good to brag to my friends about being so audacious in honoring my grandmother's memory. I thought I'd make a connection with my parents, too, but as the hog's head simmered on Andrea's stove, I felt more alone than ever. I grabbed a *kolache* from the plate of pastries I had made for Andrea as a thank-you gesture. I took a bite and realized I'd never know if this pastry was like the one Grandma used to make. I'd cobbled it together from several recipes I found online. The dough I had made with organic lemon zest and grass-fed butter, ingredients I felt certain Grandma would never have used.

When the head was fully cooked, I was not prepared for the delicious smell, which reminded me of Mom's Sunday dinners of pork roast and potatoes. We took the head out of the pot and let it cool slightly. It had cooked down to grayish-brown meat, skin, cartilage, and bone. The hog's underbite grinned up at me. We picked the meat from the skull by hand, separating it from gristle. The natural gelatin from the cartilage in the head made the meat sticky, like glue. Even though my fingertips felt coated in rubber cement, it was impossible not to pop some morsels of rich, tender meat into my mouth. It was everything pork should be.

Andrea sliced the tongue out of the jaw. Before she skinned it, I noticed the taste buds were still intact. The tongue meat was dark, more beef-like than pork.

"The tongue makes head cheese authentic," Andrea said, as she chopped off the sinewy tendons at the base of the tongue with one blow from the cleaver and began to dice the tongue into cubes.

We added a dash of vinegar and some salt and pepper to the mixing bowl of meat tidbits. Andrea also cubed some of the carrots that cooked in the stock.

"Even though it's not traditional, I think the carrots will make it more accessible to some people," she explained as if mixing in the bright orange vegetable would somehow disguise the tongue and facial meat. Maybe she was thinking of Kent's reluctance to eat offal. It nagged me that I'd strayed from replicating my grandmother's headcheese. She would never have cooked with wine, nor would she have thought to add carrots to the dish. The exact way she made head cheese was lost to me. Suddenly this whole project took on the taint of regret. My feeble attempt to recapture the past was flawed. I'd wanted a past different from the one I'd known: a past in which I'd been old enough to remember Grandma before the accident, in which I'd been brave enough to try her headcheese, in which my dad had quit drinking, and my parents were still happily married.

SARAH K. LENZ

We took the stock we cooked the head in, strained it and heated it in small saucepan to concentrate the flavor and gelatin content. Andrea lined two terrine molds with Saran wrap, spooned the meat and carrot mixture into the terrines, and poured the reduced stock over it. As soon as the head cheese set up in the refrigerator, it would be done.

*

I didn't unmold the head cheese until the next day. Kent watched as I overturned the mold on a cookie sheet. It came out a perfect, marbled brick. The pieces of meat nestled together and ranged in color from pale beige outer cheeks and mauve-tinted snout muscles to dark liver-toned tongue and were bound by the golden gelatin highlighted with bright orange carrot bits.

As soon as our two housecats caught a whiff, they crowded around me.

"See, the cats know this is delicious," I told Kent, but I said it more to reassure myself. From the far edge of the kitchen, Kent was close enough to smell it too. He decided it smelled like canned dog food. I put a slice on a plate and set it on the floor for the cats. Grandma would have cringed at this blatant waste of food. The cats were thrilled by the meaty treat.

"I don't think the cats are the best judge of taste," Kent said. "They use their tongues for toilet paper." I didn't respond to his comment, but inside I seethed. Andrea had suggested serving the headcheese with cornichons and Dijon mustard, so I pulled them from the fridge. They were accoutrements my grandmother wouldn't have employed, but which I felt would help me choke down the dish.

WHAT WILL OUTLAST ME?

I sat down at the kitchen table and took my first tentative bite. It tasted like cold pork roast. Like eating cold fried chicken, the fattiness of the meat coated the roof of my mouth. I took a bite of cornichon, and the vinegary pickle cleansed my palate. I was glad Andrea had suggested it. I felt relief, too. The texture of the jellied bits was strange in my mouth, but it wasn't disgusting. I'd succeeded.

"Here, you should try a bite." I slid the plate across the table towards Kent.

"No! I'm not going to eat it. Why won't you just accept that?"

"Not even a bite?"

"No. Just drop it." His words had a cold meanness.

I felt hurt and then anger. Why didn't he see how much this meant to me? The more I thought about it, the more I realized why I cared so much about liking the foods my family loved. It was a way to let them know *I love you*. A way to say *I like what you like too*, even if we have messy disagreements about lots of things. When I was in high school, my dad and I often sat at the kitchen table with a late-night snack of sardines, Plochman's mustard, and saltines. Because sardines are eaten bones and all, they're an acquired taste, but I acquired a taste for them for solidarity. My mother wouldn't share this with him, and maybe part of me felt that Kent not sharing headcheese with me was a bad omen for our marriage. Eating those salty, oily fish was one way I had showed my dad I loved him, but eventually I came to crave the briny dark flavor of the sardines. My freshman year of college, so homesick I could barely get out of bed, I lived off sardines and saltines not just because they were so cheap, but because they reminded me of home.

The next night Kent and I were doing dishes after an ordinary meal of pasta.

"I'm sorry that I can't eat the headcheese," he said. "I'm sorry I've disappointed you." I was surprised by his apology. Andrea was right, headcheese wasn't for everyone. My anger had faded—and it hit me that maybe I'd made headcheese out of guilt that built up all those years I'd snubbed Grandma's headcheese. Yet now seeing Kent take my old childhood stance on this dish, I felt more certain than ever that Grandma hadn't taken my refusal to eat her headcheese personally. I also knew Kent loved me and didn't need to prove it by eating headcheese. I wiped the dish suds from my hands and wrapped Kent in a hug.

"It's okay," I told him, giving him a kiss. "Look how long it finally took me to try it."

Now that I'd started my own family, I hoped my marriage would be the way I remembered my grandmother's: happy even if strapped for cash, caring and kind even after the accident. Loving someone when it's hard, when they disappoint you, or when something bad happens that changes everything, is like acquiring a taste for a food you don't like at first. You push through the hard parts because there's the hope that, in the end, it's worth it. You find nourishment.

I turned from Kent to make my lunch for the next day. I pulled the dish of headcheese out of the fridge and cut a thick slice for my sandwich. I knew I'd never make headcheese again.

WHAT WILL OUTLAST ME?

It wasn't like the sardines I'd grown to love and had fond memories of. For all the work of making it, it turned out to be a truly humbling dish, unassuming and unspectacular in its flavor. The important thing was that I'd finally had a taste, even if I were decades late to the table.

A BOOK FROM MY GRANDMA, A MESSAGE FROM THE GRAVE

The only book Grandma Lillian ever gave me was *A Tree Grows in Brooklyn*. "I thought you might like this," she said. We stood in her living room, the mottled orange and avocado shag carpet thick at our feet. When she handed it to me, the book felt antique in my hands, a brown clothbound edition, copyright 1945. Small stains dotted the front cover. Frayed around the bottom edges, the spine had ripped. I was sure it was one of her yard sale finds, but I immediately loved it because it was such a unique tome. Up until that point I only had experience with two kinds of books: hardcover library books with slick acetate covers protecting the dust jackets or cheap paperbacks Mom bought me whenever my elementary school held a Scholastic Book Fair. I plopped down on the orange, velvet club chair and began to read. Immediately, I was in over my head: "Serene was a word you could put to Brooklyn, New York. Especially in the summer of 1912." I had no idea what serene meant, but I kept going, and later when I got home, looked the word up in the dictionary. I copied the definition in pencil on the opening page: "calm, peaceful, clear, bright."

Though at ten years old, I struggled with some of the vocabulary, *A Tree Grows in Brooklyn* was the perfect book for me. It's the coming-of-age story of Frances Nolan, the daughter

WHAT WILL OUTLAST ME?

of an alcoholic father who drinks away all the family's money. Francie's tenacity and ability to see beauty everywhere helps her transcend the despair of her family's hardscrabble existence. Though rural Nebraska in the early 1990s was nothing like Brooklyn just before World War I, I had two key things in common with Francie: I was poor and my father was a drunk.

Grandma Lillian died three years later when I was only thirteen, so the memories I have of her are scant and filtered through my child's worldview. Chief in my memories are the rummage sales she took me to, which I found endlessly enchanting because each item: an old teddy bear, a warped board game, or a brightly colored silk scarf seemed to have a story—a whole life—behind it. Grandma's nearly mystical regard for objects reminds me of Frances Nolan, who "liked the pawnshop best" of all the stores in her neighborhood. It had "treasures prodigiously thrown into its barred windows." The book was an early influence of how I looked at objects in the world. Grandma Lillian was another.

When she took me to garage sales, the fact that most items cost less than dollar made me feel rich with the possibility of ownership—which took on even more significance since I knew how tight money was at home. As a teenager during the Great Depression, Grandma Lillian honored thriftiness above all. The only time I ever remember her being angry with me is when she saw that I used too many facial tissues. She called me into the bathroom, where after wiping my glasses clean, I'd deposited a fat wad of soggy tissues. She reached into the trash and grabbed them.

"Look at this waste!" she scolded me. An outburst like this was out of character for Grandma—ever since the accident I had been told—she'd been a calmer version of herself. When I was four, she had sustained a traumatic brain injury in a car wreck. My parents worried about her mental state. She often got confused and had trouble remembering things, especially where she had put household items in closets and cupboards, which she obsessively sorted and rearranged. Some patients with brain injuries become violent and more aggressive, but not Grandma. She became a faded, gentler version herself. She didn't talk much about herself, and I wonder now if it's because her memories had dissolved altogether.

The closest I ever got to her telling me about her past was when she'd open an antique, camelback trunk that held her most precious items. On rare occasions, she'd show me her collection of curiosities. Equal parts wonderful and horrifying, the trunk contained locks of her parents' hair, rattles from rattlesnakes killed on the farm in the Sandhills where she grew up, crumbling albums of photos mounted on black paper, a framed post-mortem photograph of Grandpa's three uncles who were killed by lightning, and, inexplicably in landlocked Nebraska, an extensive and carefully labelled seashell collection. Where had she gotten the shells? Had she been to the ocean? No one in my family knows. It's a trifling secret she's carried to the grave. It reminds me of all the questions I left unasked, all the things I'll never know about her.

Her chief hobby the last few years of her life was sorting through her extensive collections and labelling items she intended her children and grandchildren to have when she died. Grandma's basement looked like a giant tag sale: candy dishes, commemorative plates, china teacups, and a menagerie of figurines crowded two long rows of folding tables. She marked

WHAT WILL OUTLAST ME?

the bottom of each piece with masking tape on which she scrawled family members' names in shaky cursive.

In *A Tree Grows in Brooklyn*, Francie's inner life is often revealed through her connection to physical objects which she found beautiful. Finding beauty in the mundane is how her spirit survived poverty. For instance, at the library on the circulation desk, stood a little golden-brown pottery jug that held small sprigs of flowers, indicating the season. One summer day, the jug is full of nasturtiums. She reacts viscerally: "a head pain caught her between the eyes at the taking in of such a wonderful sight. It was something to be remembered all her life." Though it sounds sentimental, I easily imagine that for Grandma Lillian, small slices of beauty had the same effect. Was that why something as simple as a piece of pottery gave her such joy?

When she died, I received two ceramic parakeet figurines because Grandma had remembered my beloved pet budgie, Petey, and a beautiful set of champagne flutes from the 1950s etched with a starburst pattern, which my husband I used during our wedding toast. My drunk father smashed the ceramic parakeets back when I was in high school, and the champagne flutes were stolen from our storage unit during one of our cross-country moves, so over the years, my copy of *A Tree Grows in Brooklyn* has become a totem, more precious because it's the only physical object I have left from Grandma Lillian.

As the decades have gone by, I've wistfully imbued *A Tree Grows in Brooklyn* with layers of meaning far beyond what Betty Smith could have ever imagined. Though I know this is a stretch of imagination—I still entertain the thought that Grandma Krahulik meant the novel as a personal message to me. She gave it to me because it expressed all the things about being poor and having an alcoholic father, about feeling alone in the world, and about seeing cruel death all around that she couldn't say to me directly. Why else would she give me a book that really wasn't a children's book? Wouldn't she want me to see the book as a stand-in for all the things we would have talked about if I had been older, if she had lived longer? She knew our family wasn't the kind of family that talked about hard truths, but maybe fiction could speak our truth for us.

Fiction also allows us to imagine a different ending. "Sometimes it seems to me," writes Sandra Gilbert, "that as a way of thinking grief has much in common with speculative fiction. Both, after all, are about alternative lives—past, present, or future. *What if*, cries the griever, just as the sci-fi writer does. *What if* the calamity hadn't happened, the survivor broods, *what if* the dead one I loved were still alive? What would my life be like today? How would she be living? How would I?" The brief thirteen years that my life overlapped with Grandma Lillian's life were not years that either of us were in our prime. I was too young, my personality nascent, while grandma's failing mind and declining health had scoured out her personality.

Francie imagined and understood this disconnect between what we physically know of a person versus the unseen history that lies behind them. While Francie is queuing up at the day-old bakery, she sees an old man with dirty gray hair and grisly white whiskers. She watches "fascinated and revolted," as he sucked his lips up over his gums until his mouth disappeared, and his face collapsed into a grotesque figure. She surveys his tattered clothing, but the most horrifying thing is his feet. His

WHAT WILL OUTLAST ME?

shoes are broken open at the tips, so she can see his bare toes, gnarled, with hoof-like toenails. Yet Francie's imagination takes hold. She has a reverie:

He was a baby once. He must have been sweet and clean and his mother kissed his little pink toes. Maybe when it thundered at night she came to his crib and fixed his blanket better and whispered that he mustn't be afraid. Then she picked him up and put her cheek on his head and said that he was her own sweet baby. He might have been a boy like my brother, running in and out of the house and slamming the door. Then he was a young man, strong and happy. When he walked down the street, the girls smiled and turned to watch him. He smiled back and maybe he winked at the prettiest one. I guess he must have married and had children and they thought he was the most wonderful papa in the world the way he worked hard and bought them toys for Christmas. Now his children are getting old too, like him, and they have children.

So much of my grandmother's life story is lost. Even as a writer, my imagination fails to embroider the unknown details of her life. What was her courtship to Grandpa like? How did she take to new motherhood? Was she a natural, or, like me, had she been wracked with anxiety? What stands out as the key achievements in her life? Had her hopes and dreams been fulfilled? It's impossible to tell. So perhaps this is the reason I've latched onto *A Tree Grows in Brooklyn*—an ersatz stand-in for a deeper relationship to this woman who I barely knew, yet still love and miss.

For lack of this information, it's easy to imagine my grandmother as Francie. (I took it as a sign that Grandma's middle name was Frances.) Maybe this is my mind's way of filling the gaps, struggling to make a coherent narrative where there is none. "As we survivors journey into our own futures, the dead become provisional, hypothetical...if even our memories of the living blur with age, our recollections of the dead grow still more tattered, scenes from the past increasingly improbable," explains Gilbert. As the memories I have become frayed, the book becomes a stand in.

I wish Grandma Lillian could have known me as an adult. She didn't get to see me graduate from college or get married. She'll never know that I fulfilled my childhood dream of becoming a writer. She didn't get to see me become a mother. I wish Grandma could have seen my Francie-like resilience.

Though I wish Grandma had lived longer to see my successes, I'm glad she's been spared my father's tragedies. Walt Whitman echoes this sentiment in "Song of Myself," when he writes, "To die is different from what any one supposed, and luckier. / Has anyone supposed it lucky to be born? / I hasten to inform him or her it is just as lucky to die...and I know it..." Grandma's luck was that she was spared from knowing that her son's alcoholism got worse, and after a DUI, my mother divorced him. Because of his drinking, he became estranged from my sister. He has lived out retirement in a downward spiral, ending up in public housing so he could afford to keep drinking. She'll never know that at 73—the same age she was when she died—that he was arrested for another DUI and jailed in the drunk tank.

Perhaps the reason I read *A Tree Grows in Brooklyn* as a message from my dead grandmother is because the book focuses on the reality of death and preparing for it—a theme I missed as a younger reader when she was still alive. Near the end of the

WHAT WILL OUTLAST ME?

book, as Francie is preparing to go away to college and her mother has remarried, she reflects:

> *The last time of anything has the poignancy of death itself. Oh, the last time how clearly you see everything; as though a magnifying light had been turned on it. You grieve because you hadn't held it tighter when you had it everyday...Look at everything always as though you were seeing it either for the first or last time; Thus is your time on earth filled with glory."*

I had taken Grandma for granted. I hadn't held on tighter. Perhaps she's trying to teach me not to do this with my father. After all, it's a challenge to maintain closeness when, like grandma, he is fading in his elderly years. After decades of heavy drinking, his cognitive decline is noticeable. He's hard to talk to because he doesn't remember what's been said, and he has trouble hearing, even with hearing aids.

The last lesson I imagine Grandma is trying to teach me is to not numb yourself just because life is hard. Francie is always willing to look at the hard realities of her life, the ugliness of it all, and she pays attention with eyes wide open and a heart still vulnerable. She did it even when her teachers chastised her for telling too much ugly truth in her writing. Meet life on its terms. Notice as much of it as you can because you never know whether you're missing the message.

I realize it is wildly improbable that Grandma is speaking to me through a novel that's over seventy-five years old and that I have no proof she ever read, but Walter Benjamin would argue that Grandma's death has given me the authority to make exactly such a claim. "Death is the end of all story as well as the mysterious blank out of which story starts and against which it sets itself while at the same time it is what is 'impossible to tell,'" he writers in *Illuminations*. Because of death, I can't know for sure that Grandma *didn't* mean for me to take the novel as a personal message from her to me. So is my grandmother trying to communicate a message to me via Betty Smith's novel? Impossible to tell.

A skeptic might say that this is just an occupational hazard. Trained as a literary scholar in graduate school, I'm reading too much into a text, cherry-picking passages, clawing through imagery and themes to twist the work into an interpretation that is self-serving. Perhaps. Though couldn't the case as easily be made that through some premonition Grandma knew that this was her best bet at communication from the grave? For me, a book is better than a séance. Certainly, Grandma remembered I don't believe in ghosts, would never use a Ouija board, or consult a psychic to try to communicate with the dead.

The last image I remember of Grandma Lillian is of her laid out in a coffin. She looked calm, peaceful, clear, bright. Everything was so carefully arranged. She would have been proud of this attention to material detail. Her pink lipstick matched the pink roses on her dress, which caught the blush of the hand-painted roses adorning her white casket, which was covered by a huge splay of real roses—a pastel shower of pinks, peaches, and yellows.

My Quaker friends call death "the great mystery." They accept that the afterlife, if there is one, is unknown. It struck me as comforting that one could trust that the mystery was not maleficent, but just the natural order that would happen to us all. Quakers see it as another place on our journey, the one place we can never return from. Because death permanently cuts the living off from their deceased loved one, it's no wonder that our

WHAT WILL OUTLAST ME?

imaginations take hold of the smallest memories. Can I be blamed for trying to weave a message, some sort of meaning, from those few objects I have that connect me to Grandma Lillian? I know it is a futile attempt to bridge an uncrossable gulf between the living and the dead, but it's also, I think, the one thing that keeps her spirit alive.

HOLY DIMINISHMENT

I'd been in Bowling Green, Ohio six months when the dreams started. We had relocated so Kent could work on his PhD. He and I had rented an old cedar-shingled house on Elm Street. Our bedroom was so tiny only a narrow three-foot walkway separated the double bed and the walls. Its sole window looked out to the backyard and the plastics factory the next block over. The factory's smokestack exhaled fumes that smelled like the waxy plastic of cemetery flowers. I'd put a heavy gray drape over the window, which Kent said made the room coffin dark.

I woke in this room with my heart racing and my T-shirt drenched in sweat. The dreams haunted me. I imagined they were like dreams people have of their deceased loved ones, except my dreams were unpeopled. What haunted me were places. In one dream I wandered through my former apartment on North 33rd in Omaha, where Kent and I first lived when we got married. In the dream the rooms are stripped bare, but I see the details of the crown molding and mantel. The way light bounces off the eggshell walls. I stand by an upstairs window looking down at my vegetable garden. The dream consisted of nothing more, yet it left a dull, heartbroken ache in my chest.

I dreamed of other places in Omaha, too. The Idalia Street apartment, with its honeyed floorboards in the living room, hissing dining room radiator, and porcelain octagon tile in the

WHAT WILL OUTLAST ME?

bathroom. In my dreams the apartments were always empty. I dreamed of the efficiency rental on Izard Street with its window seat overlooking a backyard of mulberry trees. Purple berries stained the sidewalk with hundreds of bruises. The rotten fruit gave off a pungent and cloying smell, but when picked ripe from the tree, the berries made great pies.

"Better than sex pies," I jokingly called them back then. Now I didn't even talk about sex anymore, let alone joke about it.

*

The move had been hard. Fresh out of grad school and struggling to find work in my field, I ended up with a shit job in downtown Toledo at a restaurant called Pizza Papalis. It was a forty-mile commute, so I tried to work double shifts to save on gas. The empty hours between lunch and dinner I spent at the public library a few blocks away. As I wandered the stacks, I smelled book musk and library paste. It mingled with the pizza sauce and onion odors from my uniform—a tight baby-T designed to show off my breasts. I missed the starched white tuxedo shirt I wore at my last job at an upscale steakhouse. I also missed school.

It was the first fall since kindergarten that I wouldn't be starting classes. I envied Kent, and I was frustrated by my job prospects. What had been the point of grad school when my current job didn't even require a high school diploma? I went to the library and checked out stacks of books, thinking one of them could tell me why I was unhappy, haunted by old places. I checked out Gaston Bachelard's *The Poetics of Space* and Rebecca Solnit's *A Field Guide to Getting Lost*.

SARAH K. LENZ

I spent my days off from Pizza Papalis reading. Cold wind rattled our poorly insulated windows. I stayed cozy, wearing my pajamas all day, brewing pots of tea. While reading Bachelard, I stumbled across an explanation for my haunting dreams: "After we are in the new house, memories of other places we have lived in come back to us. Houses that were lost forever continue to live on in us; they exist in us in order to live again. We consider the past, and a sort of remorse at not having lived profoundly enough in the old house fills our hearts, comes up from the past, overwhelms us." His words chilled me. I dreamed about those apartments in Omaha because they were where I'd fallen in love with Kent, where I'd been happy. When I was living in those rooms, I'd taken that contentment and joy for granted. I'd assumed such happiness would always be with me.

The next morning on my commute to Pizza Papalis, I drove north on I-75. Before merging with downtown traffic, I crossed I-80. When I saw the westbound sign, I fantasized about taking the interchange, pointing the nose of my Geo Metro west and not stopping until I reached Nebraska. As I passed under the green and white exit sign to I-80, I started crying. *The only reason I'm in Ohio is for Kent, and he doesn't want me here.*

My unhappiness was rooted in loneliness, and loneliness is a spatial problem of isolation. I barely saw Kent. He spent his late-night hours studying at the campus library or a coffee shop. One night I tracked him down. He was at Panera Bakery, studying at a table with three coed classmates. When he introduced me to them, they didn't smile or offer their hands. I was an intruder; I didn't belong.

WHAT WILL OUTLAST ME?

The next afternoon during my shift, I had a panic attack. My heart raced, my palms sweated, and my breastbone ached. The fear of losing my job was great enough that I pretended nothing was wrong. Balancing a large pepperoni pizza on my tray, I smiled and put it on the guests' table. I felt faint. Sheer will kept me from cracking my façade.

I thought back to the desperation a couple of months ago. That winter, unemployment rates in Northwest Ohio were at a national high. I had fifty job applications out, but Pizza Papalis was the only one that had called back. The restaurant was a Detroit-based chain that had just opened its first Toledo location. When I was offered the job, I was grateful because we were living solely off Kent's paltry graduate stipend. Money grew so tight that I felt sick to my stomach when I spent $12 to buy two desperately needed sweaters at Goodwill. We survived by eating cornmeal mush and eggs. The first day of training, a level three blizzard roared outside, but I had braved the slick, snow packed roads and white-out conditions for fear I'd lose the job if I didn't show up. At orientation, I had sat with twenty other new employees in an unfinished cement-floored dining room. Snow swirled outside. The motion and glare made my eyes hurt and my head feel dizzy. The dirty slush of snow melting off our boots pooled at our feet. The general manager, Brent, blond and red-faced, had held a three-inch stack of papers in his hands. He waved it above his head.

"You see this?" he screamed. "Every sheet of paper is an application from someone who wants your job. One mistake, one misstep, and you don't work here."

*

SARAH K. LENZ

Kent and I sat parked in the near-empty lot of Meijer Supermarket. I held a grocery list carefully crafted to stay within our small budget. The wind pitched storm clouds through the sky. Tumbleweeds rolled across the blacktop. The car rocked and quivered in the gusts of wind. In the closed space of the Geo Metro, our unhappiness hovered between us, but instead of trying to ignore it, like I did with the panic attacks, I found the courage to speak.

"Are you okay?" I asked Kent. "It's like you're not really here. You're stuck inside your head."

"I have a lot on my plate with school. It's harder than I thought it would be. What's wrong with *you*?"

"I hate this place. I have nothing but you, and you're not even here." I began crying, hating how whiny and needy I sounded.

"I don't know what to tell you, Hon. I don't know what you want." He tried to hug me, but my seatbelt got in the way. I held myself rigid where my shoulder ached from carrying heavy pizza trays and stared out into the dark, almost empty parking lot as another tumbleweed rolled by.

"You need to do something. You mope around the house all day in your pajamas, doing nothing."

"That's not true. I read."

He shot me a look like that didn't count. "I'm just saying, you don't seem to know what you want."

What I wanted was to go somewhere else, somewhere I had been happy, but those places didn't exist anymore.

*

WHAT WILL OUTLAST ME?

I kept dreaming of other places where I'd lived. I dreamed of the Nebraska farm where I grew up. It's spring, almost Easter. I stand by the window in the brooder house, looking out at a budding stand of cottonwoods. Behind me hundreds of day-old chicks cheep a high-pitched cacophony from their bed of sawdust under a heat lamp. I scoop a yellow chick up in my hands, draw it to my face, and inhale, smelling salt and sunlight.

I awoke from that dream with an inexplicable longing like a stomachache. The dream felt important, like an omen, but I felt silly trying to put it into words, so I didn't tell Kent about the dreams. A few days later, I read *In a Field Guide to Getting Lost* that "Place possesses you in its absence, takes on another life. The places inside matter as much as the ones outside. It is as though in the way places stay with you and that you long for them they become deities."

*

In an effort to make new friends, Kent took me to a house party that a classmate hosted. We drank cheap beer. Kent introduced me to James, a fellow grad student, who looked like a crunchy-granola hippy with his long ponytail and thrift-store clothing. He was a devoted environmentalist. I told him about the organic vegetable gardening I'd done in the other places I'd lived.

"Did you compost?" he asked. When I told him no, he explained how terrible it is for the environment to throw food scraps away. "Everyone should compost. If I get some worms, I could vermicompost in my apartment."

"Or you could use my backyard."

He liked my idea and agreed to maintain a compost heap in a corner of my yard if he could dump his kitchen scraps there too.

"When I was in Pennsylvania," he said. "I learned a lot about the local food movement from the Quaker Earthcare Committee I belonged to."

"Quakers?" I vaguely remembered Quakers from some TV show I'd watched. "Are they the ones that have completely silent church services?"

"Sort of. In a meeting for worship, we believe in sitting in expectant silence for a message from God. If you receive a message, then you stand and speak it. Some people feel so overwhelmed when a message comes that they physically quake, hence the name."

"That's fascinating," I said, but I wasn't sure I meant it. I was curious, yes, but I was also a little drunk. I'd quit going to church years ago. After Grandpa Harvey died, sermons felt more like judgmental damnation than loving spiritual instruction.

"If you're interested, there's a Quaker meeting in Toledo we could go to. I don't own a car, though, and I haven't found anybody to take me."

"I could take you," I blurted. It was the beer talking.

When Sunday morning arrived, I didn't want to go to Quaker church, but I didn't want to break my word with James either and wreck our new friendship.

The Toledo Friends' Meeting met in a small cottage. We arrived a few minutes late, and the room had already fallen hush. A dozen people sat in a loose circle on couches and folding

WHAT WILL OUTLAST ME?

chairs. Most had their eyes closed. I found an open seat at one end of a blue couch next to a picture window that looked out at bare-branched trees. I felt uncomfortable. I stared at my shoes. I noted the women next to me who seemed to be breathing louder than necessary. Just get through this. *It's only an hour*, I told myself. I scratched an itch on my ankle. As the clock ticked on, my rambling thoughts had latched onto one question:

What the hell are you doing here? What are you doing here?

I'd grown up in a fundamentalist evangelical Christian church that believed the only path to salvation was being born again. Grandpa Harvey had attended a Presbyterian church that didn't take such a hardline position of salvation. A few weeks before he died, I'd attempted to evangelize him. He refused to say the Sinner's Prayer with me. Then he died. The pastor at our church told me that because he hadn't been saved, Grandpa was now suffering eternity in hell.

I had tried everything I could to save him. While I was away at college, I'd written him proselytizing letters, but none of it had worked. I was tired of hearing that God has a reason for everything. That's when I stopped going to church. Since then, I knew organized religion wasn't for me. *What the hell are you doing here? Why are you here?* I kept asking myself.

Then from somewhere in the silence an answer rose up: *You're here because you want your life to have meaning.* As soon as that thought formed, a stout, elderly woman stood up. Her hands quivered like bird wings. Her voice wavered as she said, "Spirituality is for those of us who refuse to believe our lives are meaningless."

During the car ride home, I explained to James what had happened. How it seemed like that woman had known exactly what I was thinking and then said it aloud.

"That happens in meeting all the time," James said. "We even have a phrase for it. We say, 'Friend spoke my mind.'"

*

I dreamed about the hen house from my childhood. Wild sparks of dust moats swirl down from the window onto the golden hay. A row of broody, bronze-feathered hens sit in nesting boxes. I cup my hand inside my sleeve in case the hen pecks and reach under her feathered chest. The eggs make a dull clink as they tumble together but don't break. I draw a warm egg out from under the hen. She erupts with a stream of angry clucks.

*

The next Sunday, I went back to the Toledo Friends' Meeting with James. This time the silence felt less fraught, and we stayed for tea afterward. The group had been reading a Pendlehill pamphlet called "Hallowing Our Diminishments." The woman who'd spoke at that last meeting, who'd introduced herself as Judy, explained to me that they had set aside this time after worship to discuss the reading. Another woman, Janet, who had white hair, and wore a linen tunic started reading. Her voice was surprisingly strong given her tiny frame:

If you are to hallow diminishment, it is necessary to fill your life with interesting, new, self-appointed work. Abandon yourself to the double thread of your life: the thread of inward development, through which your affections are formed; and the thread of outward success, which is where the forces of the universe converge.

WHAT WILL OUTLAST ME?

No one spoke for a long time. I took a sip of peppermint tea. I wasn't familiar with the word diminishment as a catch-all term for maladies, illness, grief, and loss, but the accuracy of it rushed in. Our move to Ohio had been a diminishment. I'd lost my sense of purpose, I'd lost my academic community of friends, I'd lost a comfortable home, and I'd lost the secure happiness of my marriage. A lump formed in my throat. I took another sip of tea, so I wouldn't cry.

Finally, Janet spoke. "I found comfort in this. That even as I physically diminish, there is still valuable work I can do." Her hearing aid screeched, as if to punctuate her point. She cocked her head and fiddled with it.

"I love the idea of the double thread," said Judy. "The physical and spiritual aren't separate."

Suddenly, I thought about all those chicken dreams. Could raising chickens be the new, self-appointed work I needed to get out of my depression?

The next day between lunch and dinner shifts at Pizza Papalis, I went to the library in search of poultry-raising manuals. After skimming a couple of books, I realized it was even simpler than I thought. They just needed a small coop—at least four square feet per bird—where they could safely roost from predators at night and that was equipped with a nesting box where they could lay eggs.

*

After a long day of classes, Kent came home to find me reading in the overstuffed chair in the living room, exactly where he'd left me.

"You haven't moved," he said. "What have you been doing?"

"This," I said. It was true I'd been reading most of the day, but I'd also been searching online for potential chicken coops, and I'd found a woman in Toledo who was selling a rabbit hutch that might work as a chicken house.

He rolled his eyes in disgust and stomped off to his home office where I found him at his desk, checking email. I flopped down on the blue loveseat behind him. Kent's office looked like a ten-year-old boy had decorated it. Plastic Superman and Batman figurines stood on the shelves next to his elaborate Lego creations. Like me, he'd been reaching for his childhood.

"I want to raise chickens," I blurted.

He swiveled his desk chair around and faced me, incredulous.

"I need a project. You have school. What have I got?" I said. I felt like I was begging a parent for permission.

He listed the reasons why my request was unrealistic.

"We live in town. They have nowhere to sleep. Where do you even get chickens? What would they eat? You haven't thought this through, Hon."

But I had. Researching Bowling Green City Code revealed that as long as they didn't roam free, chickens could legally be kept within city limits. Then I told Kent about how I'd found a rabbit hutch to use as a coop. I explained that I'd buy the chicks at the farm supply store, where I'd also get their chicken kibble, but that they ate bugs and kitchen scraps too. By the time I'd pled my case, he realized that I went from asking him

WHAT WILL OUTLAST ME?

if I could raise chickens to telling him I was going to whether he liked it or not.

Knowing he was defeated, he asked me one last question, "What if a chicken goes radioactive, grows to five feet tall, and attacks us?"

I cracked a smile and knew I'd won. In that moment, I saw a glimmer of the way Kent was before the PhD program when he made me laugh all the time. I realized it'd been a long time since I'd heard Kent joke, and it hit me that he had been diminished by this move too.

*

The next day I followed MapQuest directions to a crummy neighborhood south of University of Toledo where the rabbit hutch woman from Craigslist lived. An overweight and mousy-looking woman answered the door and told me to meet her around the side of the house. She swung open the gate to the sagging privacy fence, letting me into a domestic junkyard.

I followed the woman through her yard, picking my way around a fifty-foot coil of hose, a pile of rusted metal posts, a row of broken push lawnmowers, and a heap of bicycles, I thought maybe this was her way of hallowing a diminishment. *Is junk picking her self-appointed work?* We reached the hutch at the back corner of the yard.

"I just don't think that it'll work for chickens," the woman said, "but here it is." Her breath puffed slightly from the effort of clearing us a path to get to the hutch. She picked up an old rake, an empty gas can, and an overturned five-gallon bucket.

"I used to raise and show rabbits, but I just don't have the time anymore."

"This could work," I said. I would board up half of the hutch to make the walls of the coop, the other half could be the run.

"You're asking $25?"

"Well, I could let it go for $15, but just don't tell my husband."

"I'll take it."

*

A week later, in a carton shaped like a McDonald's Happy Meal box, I brought three chicks home from the farm supply store. Their fuzzy bodies ranged in color from buttery yellow to strawberry blonde. I put them in the laundry room in a big cardboard box under a heat lamp. They pecked greedily at their mash, then curled up in a downy heap no bigger than a tennis ball and fell asleep.

*

By May, the chickens had grown as big as pigeons. Once they grew rough patches of pinfeathers, I moved them from the laundry room to their rabbit hutch. A few weeks later, Kent surprised me with a gift for the chickens. Because our yard had no fence, he built me a movable chicken pen from 2"- by- 2"s and chicken wire, forming an eight-foot square fence, light enough to move to a fresh patch of grass every day. It was good to see him back in his woodshop, working on a project that had nothing to do with his PhD program.

That night Kent and I ate dinner on the back patio while the chickens grazed in their new pen a few feet away, scratching for bugs in the lawn. Beyond them rose the industrial rumble of the plastics factory, but even the noise of clanging forklifts

WHAT WILL OUTLAST ME?

couldn't drown out the chickens' contented clucking. After dinner, we sat watching them for a long time, mesmerized by their simple, mindful natures.

"Thank you," I said. That's when I told Kent about the terrible dreams I'd been having and how homesick I was for Omaha.

"Why don't you take a trip back?" he asked.

"With what money?"

"Put it on my credit card."

I thought about it, but then realized my old haunts wouldn't be the same. The memories I had of them were enough and would remain—fixed and perfect—the idealized version I invented in an attempt to pin happiness in place. I didn't need to explain this to Kent. He knew homesickness too. I looked across the patio table at him. The glow from the setting sun sparkled in the gold flecks of his green eyes.

He smiled. "I want you to be happy," he said.

He took my hand and squeezed it.

*

Slowly the despair and loneliness I'd felt melted away. I was grieving for a place, and like grief for a person, the pain ebbed before it gradually faded. It was hard to pinpoint the moment when I was no longer so sad. The chickens helped by giving me a reason to get out of bed. Each morning at dawn, I went to the coop to let them out. (I padlocked their coop shut every evening to protect them from raccoons.) They rushed the door in a klutzy stampede that always made me smile. By summer I was able to quit Pizza Papalis when I got a new job teaching middle schoolers in a reading enrichment program. The following fall,

I finally got a job teaching writing at the university. I kept going to Quaker meetings and that helped too.

Quakers believe that that if we listen and are open, we can experience the Divine through any channel. One July morning, I found the first egg one of my hens had laid. From its bed of straw in the nesting box, it seemed a miracle. I held it in my hand, marveling at its perfect oval, feeling its smooth weight and gentle warmth, like something full of hope and promise. Its pale brown shell seemed luminescent. This egg had been made by my hen. Her body contained everything she needed to produce an egg. The chickens gave me the gift of noticing things again—of feeling the richness of being alive and of being connected to other living things. The Quakers reminded me that there is that double thread—that anything can be hallowed.

After four years in Ohio, Kent finished his PhD program. (James had moved away the year before after he finished his Master's program—and it was clear the compost pile was suffering in his absence.) A week before we were to move away, my closest Quaker friends came to my house for a going-away party. I knew our next move, to Georgia, would be another hard one. I was leaving a deeply authentic spiritual community, lots of new friends, a fulfilling teaching job, and a well-established organic garden. There was another diminishment, too. The chickens—who were so old now they'd stopped laying eggs—were going to be butchered soon.

Before my half dozen Quaker friends and I dug into the covered dishes everyone had brought for potluck, we decided to spend time in silent worship. We circled up in my living room and went into the silence. Listened. After years of silent worship, I'd found a soul-quenching depth I longed for in the

WHAT WILL OUTLAST ME?

quiet. After about twenty-minutes, Judy broke the silence with a message:

"I see us all kneeling on the ground. Bending down and wrapping up something. I get closer, and it is Sarah. We are wrapping her in a cocoon with our love. Like a butterfly, she'll go dormant before she spreads her wings again. There is nothing to fear. When she comes out of the cocoon again, there is Light. So much Light."

I peeked my eye open to glance down at the butterfly tattoo on my bicep. I'd gotten it years ago, before Grandpa Harvey died, before I met Kent, before I moved to Ohio. I chose the butterfly tattoo because I was fascinated by a parable from *Zorba the Greek*. A little boy finds a butterfly struggling and thrashing in effort to get out of its cocoon. The boy helps peel the chrysalis off, and the insect comes out hideously bloated with shriveled wings, and soon dies. It's only through the fight to get out of the cocoon that the butterfly's wings become strong enough to fly.

The hard work of transformation, I realized, was another way to hallow diminishment. I closed my eyes again, and as I let the silence sweep over me again, I thought, *Friend spoke my mind.*

A CASE FOR RUBBERNECKING

We enjoy contemplating the most precise images of things whose actual sight is painful to us, such as the forms of the vilest animals and of corpses. –Aristotle

The first time I rubbernecked and saw a corpse was on Christmas Day. I was riding with my husband and in-laws to a family Christmas celebration. It was midmorning, and suddenly the freeway ahead of us clogged with cars, an unbroken string of red brake lights. Sam, who was driving, was forced to stop the Toyota Highlander.

"Look at these idiots. They don't know how to drive," Sam said.

We thought the heavy traffic was just holiday related until my mother-in-law checked the traffic on her phone.

"It says there's an accident one mile ahead."

"Damn rubberneckers!" Sam pounded the steering wheel. "If they'd just pay attention and drive, this wouldn't happen."

When a space opened in front of the Highlander, Sam punched the accelerator, only to slam on the brakes hard the next moment. After twenty-minutes of this, we arrived at the scene of the accident. Whirling red and silver ambulance lights

WHAT WILL OUTLAST ME?

brightened the dull winter landscape. As we inched by, we craned our heads, hungry to see what caused our delay. A vehicle had smashed through a metal guardrail and careened down the heavily treed ravine. The guardrail lay on the ground like a jagged bit of tinsel. The ravine was deep; we couldn't see the car. From behind the crumpled guardrail four EMTs appeared bearing a stretcher, the body on it shrouded by a sheet so white it seemed to glow as it caught in the wind. It chilled me to see the body being borne out of the wreck. This was the first time I'd rubbernecked and seen a corpse. Even though it was covered, it still had a haunting power. I wondered about the nature of injuries. *Had there been a lot of blood?* I adjusted my shoulders, so my seatbelt hugged me tighter. Sam's aggressive, erratic driving often scared me, and I thought what most rubberneckers must think: *Thank God that wasn't me.* Strapped safely under a seatbelt, it occurred to me that whoever loved the person under that sheet wouldn't be having much of a Christmas, but even that shred of sympathy seemed false. The deceased was an anonymous stranger. I didn't care about their death, though a nagging feeling told me I should—if only because of how easily I could become a traffic fatality, too.

For the rest of the journey no one said a word about the accident. Later that same afternoon, as I ate oysters and drank beer at our family celebration, I kept thinking about it. That scene stayed with me: the stretcher, the white sheet, the EMTs in their crisp uniforms. What I experienced was *schadenfreude*, and now I felt awful about it, remembering that when we passed the scene my blood pounded with a thrilling rush that now struck me as unseemly. A shiver of shame passed through me.

The shame I felt at rubbernecking shouldn't have surprised me. It's loathsome behavior. Blamed for slowing traffic, we even believe that by their gawking, rubberneckers increase the victim's anguish. Rubbernecking shares too much with voyeurism because it's staring at something you know you shouldn't. Sam's response—"Damn rubberneckers!"—is the common one, yet he too, turned his gaze to the accident. No one wants to admit to rubbernecking, but we've all done it. We can't help ourselves.

Our brains are hardwired for it. Neuroscientists have noted that whenever we see a novel sight our brain floods with dopamine. This is the exact response the brain produces in reaction to pleasure. This is the chemical your brain releases when you hit the jackpot, have an orgasm, or get tipsy on alcohol. Though the aftermath of an accident should seem repulsive, we're drawn to its novelty. When we see something startling, it excites us with that hit of dopamine.

Rubbernecking is rife with contradictions. Rosemarie Garland-Thompson points out this paradoxical predicament: "The extraordinary excites but alarms us; the ordinary assures but bores us. We want surprise, but perhaps even more we want to tame that pleasurable astonishment, to domesticate the strange sight. Rubbernecking can be fleeting because as soon as we take in the alarming sight, and make visual sense of it, we regain equilibrium." Rubbernecking focuses our curiosity and fascination on moments when order and moral imperatives are momentarily turned askew. Perhaps its fleeting quality imbues it with more mystery than it would have otherwise.

The problem with rubbernecking is that it can lead to the rash rationalization that puts the scene in its place, robbing it of

WHAT WILL OUTLAST ME?

its power. We victim-blame so we can feel safe. If they *deserved it*, if they *got what was coming to them*, then it can't happen to me. "Must have been a drunk driver," we say, or something equally dismissive.

*

On a fourth-grade fieldtrip, my best friend Matthew Dockhorn taught me the Roadkill Game. Whoever correctly identified the highest number of dead animals on the shoulder won. In central Nebraska we delighted in encountering deer, raccoons, and the occasional coyote or rattlesnake.

"It's a skunk," I screamed, only to be disappointed and sad when the bus whizzed past the carcass and the lack of a bushy tail told me I was wrong. It was someone's tuxedo cat, one that looked too much like my own cat, Muffin. Sometimes we couldn't tell what former animal we saw, the corpse having rotted to shreds of fur, hide, and bone. Playing the Roadkill Game shared rubbernecking's voyeurism and made the otherwise monotonous bus ride pass quickly. Though it lacked the surprise element of true rubbernecking, it made up for it with the adrenaline aroused by competition.

As an adult I find the Roadkill Game distasteful, but still, from time to time I find myself playing it alone. Since my husband and I are academics with university jobs 130 miles apart, at least once a month I drive from my home in Milledgeville to his in Statesboro along US 441 and I-16, dull stretches of highway flanked by unyielding acres of pine trees. In Georgia, the roadkill sightings are more diverse and plentiful than in my home state. Nine-banded armadillos split like plastic jugs, possums shred apart like discarded feather boas, wild turkeys' wings splay like Japanese fans, and deer bloat to the size and shape of propane tanks, their gaseous decay accelerated by Southern heat. Black vultures and turkey buzzards circle and swoop, greedy for the roadside buffet. As my car passes a venue of vultures, they lift their heads. One clasps a chunk of bloody red flesh in its beak, reminding me of what Maggie Nelson refers to as "the situation of meat." She writes, "The spectre of our eventual becoming object—of our (live) flesh one day turning into (dead) meat—is a shadow that accompanies us throughout our lives."

At thirty-three, I'm still young enough that my few deceased contemporaries have all been claimed by traffic accidents. The roadkill offers me a poignant reminder that I will die. My "situation" may one day translate into meat. Given a chance, those buzzards would rip out my entrails and feast on my flesh.

Lately, I find myself gawking at rubberneckers caught on film. Since photography became a common journalistic and artistic medium, photographers have captured all sorts of scenes that induce rubbernecking. Photographers and rubberneckers have a lot in common. In an introductory photography class I took, a classmate religiously chased ambulances to complete his homework. His contact sheets were full of thumbnail-sized car wrecks, fire trucks, and police officers.

Other "photorubberneckers" have made names for themselves through documenting the grotesque. When Mathew Brady's exhibition, "The Dead of Antietam"—a show of silver-gelatin prints depicting the dead Civil War soldiers littering the battlefield—opened to the public, it wasn't the dead bodies that fascinated a *New York Times* reporter so much as the expressions of spectators in the gallery. The anonymous 1862 article described the crowd:

> *You find them bending over photographic views of that fearful battlefield, taken immediately after the action. Of all objects of horror, one would think the battlefield should stand preeminent, that it should bear away the palm of repulsiveness. But, on the contrary, there is a terrible fascination about it that draws one near these pictures and makes him loth [sic] to leave them. You will see hushed, reverent groups standing around these weird copies of carnage, bending down to look in the pale faces of the dead, chained by the strange spell that dwells in dead men's eyes.*

By taking the accident, the war, or the crime scene out of context, and placing it on the gallery wall, these photographers give us permission to gawk. They also extract a startling beauty out of our shared mortality.

Another photographer, New Yorker Arthur Fellig (known as "Weegee"), was *the* iconic photographer-cum-ambulance chaser in the '30s and '40s. He owed his moniker—a phonetic play on the fortune-telling board game—to his prophetic ability to arrive with loaded camera at scenes of crime ahead of the authorities. Some dismiss his work as predecessor to the modern tabloid, but his most telling and poignant photographs aren't of victims but of the crowds huddled around them. In one photograph entitled "Brooklyn School Children See Gambler Murdered in the Street" (1941), the emotions on the faces of the fifteen onlookers evoke the range of expressions depicted in one of Norman Rockwell's cornier tableaus. In the center of the frame, a chubby, brown-eyed girl stares with rapt attention, while to the left, a towheaded boy breaks into a toothy grin. The moment Weegee captured with his Speed Graphic is one of eager tumult and enthusiastic chaos. Behind the children eagerly jostling for a better view, a middle-aged woman wails, caught with eyes closed and mouth gaping. Of the fifteen witnesses, her face alone conveys grief. The other expressions are bent toward amusement, making a murder seem spontaneous as a carnival sideshow. This is why rubberneckers embarrass us and make us nervous: they have no sense of propriety or decorum. They parade our worst instincts.

When Weegee exhibited this photo two years later for a show at the Museum of Modern Art, he retitled the image "Their First Murder." This drew attention away from the victim and towards the onlookers. It's no longer a photo of a crime, but an image that documents the pleasures of witnessing violence.

I find myself passing judgment. The blond boy with the wide smile, the exhilarated look on his face, *what type of monster is that?* But given time to reflect I withdraw the judgment. The act of rubbernecking itself isn't to blame, nor is the rubberneckers. For true rubbernecking to occur, the spectator must be caught off guard. This results in surprising and often overwhelming reactions—reactions beyond our power to censor.

Still, it can be hard to see merit in rubberneckers, especially when they do nothing to stop a brutality, for example, at a lynching. American lynchings featured all the elements required for rubbernecking: sudden public violence with a gruesome central focal element. a dead body dangling from a noose. In 2000, curator James Allen opened *Without Sanctuary*, an exhibition that gathers over a hundred photographs of

WHAT WILL OUTLAST ME?

lynchings taken between 1882 and 1965. Most of the photos were originally reproduced as postcards, something the spectators could take home with them, a souvenir. Why keep a picture of something so terrible? Allen thinks these people needed the postcards to act as "a receptacle for a collective sinful self." The commonplaceness of tourists' postcards disperses the horror, turning it into spectacle. As the horrific scene is reproduced over and over, the original abomination diffuses.

One morning during the fall semester, I present Allen's online slide show of the lynching photographs to my English Composition students. I dim the room. Limp, dead bodies appear and flicker on the screen. The corpses hang from telephone poles and bridges like banners or flags. Here is the aftermath of a manhunt, the captured prey proudly displayed. We look at a tree with a cluster of four dead black men hanging, and I think, *like a bevy of pheasants.*

We look at the corpse of a black man dangling from rope that's lashed to his broken wrists, which are cracked back at a right angle. He is strung up on a tall, wooden tripod the same way you'd tie a hog for butchering. His flayed ribs show deep gashes from whipping. His head arches up to heaven in that last moment he gasped for breath. In the foreground of the picture, there they are: the rubberneckers, white men circled in conversation. Allen's voice cracks over the speaker: "It wasn't the corpse that bewildered me as much as the canine-thin faces of the pack, lingering in the woods, circling after the kill."

From my seat at the front of the room, I watch my students watch the slide show. The light from the screen plays across their young faces, flashing light, dark and then light again.

SARAH K. LENZ

Milledgeville has a population nearly evenly split between Blacks and whites, but the student body of Georgia College, where I teach, is 80 percent white and 8 percent Black.

My students remind me of Weegee's spectators. Though no one looks gleeful, there's a range of expressions. Some students look bored, and their stares are blank. Others look perplexed. Then I see her. Jasmine sits in the front row. Tears well in her eyes and threaten to drop on her light brown cheeks. Self-identified as mixed-race, she's the only person of color in the class. When the slideshow ends, she is furious with me.

Later when Jasmine visits me during office hours, she says, "I don't think it was right of you to show those disgustingly vivid African-American killings." My stomach turns. I regret upsetting her so much, but I still think viewing these photos has merit. She sees me as just another rubbernecker, exploiting the spectacle.

"I think you crossed a line," she tells me. I hope she doesn't start crying again. I apologize. I am sorry that my classroom became a place where she lost control of her emotions. I explain my pedagogy, reminding her that the point of the exercise was to help us think critically about human rights violations. I remind her what Allen said in the video: "Studying these photographs has engendered in me a caution of whites, of the majority, of the young, of religion, of the accepted." But this is problematic. In *Regarding the Pain of Others*, Susan Sontag discusses why viewing violent scenes doesn't prevent future violence. It makes the viewers feel invulnerable. Jasmine was upset because she was the only person in the room who could imagine lynching as a potential threat. The rest of us, shrouded

WHAT WILL OUTLAST ME?

in privilege granted only by the color of skin, couldn't entertain the notion of a lynch mob ever killing us or our kin.

When my class discusses the slide show, a blonde sorority girl says, "I think these photos really show us how far we've come. We're not racist anymore. It's horrible that this happened, but I think we can all be grateful things like this don't happen anymore."

The semester ended. A few months later, Trayvon Martin was shot and killed. A few months after that, Eric Garner was killed. A few months after that, Michael Brown was shot and killed. All these men were black. All these men were unarmed. All these men died at the hands of white men. Some of the killers were police officers, some weren't, but all claimed self-defense. There were rubberneckers present. I wonder if the students I showed the lynching photographs to were changed by it. Maybe they see some connection to those images and the ones that are all over the news right now.

When eighteen-year-old Michael Brown was killed in Ferguson, Missouri, in August 2014, the images of the riots that erupted in the St. Louis suburb were in the news for over a month. One newsfeed uploaded pictures citizens (not journalists) took. One woman snapped a selfie after being tear gassed, showing her red, snot-crusted eyes. Another lifted her shirt, exposing billy-club bruises from police brutality. The mainstream media released photographs of the streets enveloped in clouds of tear gas, SWAT teams in riot gear beating back angry crowds. I scrolled through pages and pages of these images. At first it seemed surreal, and then, it didn't. This happened in the Midwest, where I'm from. It could happen anywhere. We're drawn to stare at—and even crave—the sight of these brutalities because we're seeking some sort of gritty veracity. We want to know what really happened.

Sometimes there's a danger in this. When we repetitively view violent images, we inoculate ourselves against empathy. It's easy to come to the swift conclusion, "Phew! Glad that could never happen to me." If we dig deeper, though, we can see this for what it is: a shallow defense mechanism. However, I believe in rubbernecking's power to catch us off guard, to force us to look at things too difficult to view otherwise, and from which, empathy can arise. We might begin by casting the victim as Other, but it's possible—if we really look—to see their suffering, and be moved to true empathy, imagining ourselves taking their place.

Cynics deny that violence can effect positive change in the world. It's a reductive view that sees violence as only begetting more violence. Elaine Scarry argues, "surely what we should wish for is a world where the vulnerability of the beholder is equal to or greater than the vulnerability of the person beheld, a world where the…tumult of staring is a prelude to acts that will add to the beauty already in the world…acts like repairing an injury or a social injustice."

Whether you believe violence can lead to redemption or not boils down to faith. Rubbernecking, is after all, only a small sliver of visual truth—one that can change from moment to moment. As far as I know, no one else in the car on that Christmas day experienced seeing the corpse the way I did. To call my experience a spiritual reckoning might not be the correct terminology, but it's not far off.

Iris Murdoch believed spiritual power arose from the times rubbernecking rips our conceited veil. "We experience the

WHAT WILL OUTLAST ME?

Sublime when we confront the awful contingency of nature or of human fate and return to ourselves with a proud shudder of rational power. How abject we are, and yet our consciousness is of an infinite value," she explains. The failure I saw in my students to take lynching photographs seriously was exactly as Murdoch described it: "By opening our eyes we do not necessarily see what confronts us. We are anxiety-ridden animals. Our minds are continually active, fabricating an anxious, usually self-preoccupied, often falsifying veil which partially conceals the world." But she reminds us it doesn't always have to be that way: "Anything which alters consciousness in the direction of unselfishness, objectivity, and realism is to be connected with virtue."

The next semester, after studying film clips of Philip Zimbardo's 1971 Stanford Prison Experiment, I try to prove to my new students how easy it is to succumb to groupthink, how hard it is to stand up to the crowd, and how difficult it is to push against authority. As Zimbardo proved, people will fall into prescribed roles (even evil ones) with alacrity. I show my students the photos of American soldiers torturing detainees at Abu Ghraib during the Iraq War. We look at Specialist Charles Graner as he crouches above a corpse covered with contusions in a body bag. Graner beams up at the camera, hand raised in a thumbs-up. We see him again with his girlfriend, and fellow soldier, Lynndie England. This time they are posed—arms around each other—standing behind a naked pyramid of prisoners. The detainees, with heads shrouded in black sandbags, are forced into positions of sexual molestation. Graner and England smile, and again raise hands in thumbs-up.

Just like the souvenir postcards of the lynchings, these photographs are trophies.

My students show no emotional reaction to these torture images, but I'm not concerned. Again, for rubbernecking to work, it must have the element of the unexpected. Sontag mentions it's a characteristic of modernity that people feel they can anticipate their own experience before it happens. I gave my students that opportunity when I asked them each to sign a "trigger warning" statement, in which they were warned they would be required to look at disturbing images. Evan, a clean-cut pre-med says, "I know we all say we'd never do what Graner did, but now I'm not sure. Not after seeing what those guys in the Stanford Prison experiment did. I'd probably do the same thing." Seeing the atrocities another human being committed scares us because we are human beings, too. We get uneasy knowing the cruelty we're capable of enacting.

*

About fifteen years ago, I witnessed a car accident. I drove an egg-shaped Geo Metro at the time and was stopped at a traffic light on a one-way street. For some reason, I hesitated for a moment when the light turned green and the SUV in the left lane next to me made it into the intersection before I did. As the SUV crossed into the center of the intersection, a car coming from the cross street on my right zoomed in front of me, running its red light, and narrowly missing my front fender. It crashed into the SUV ahead of me. The SUV rolled as easily as an aluminum pop can, then slid twenty yards before it came to a stop, upside down. The SUV driver dangled upside down, tethered in place by his seatbelt. I stared at him. I didn't see him move, and I was terrified the impact had killed him. Other

WHAT WILL OUTLAST ME?

motorists and pedestrians joining me made a ring of rubberneckers. The paramedics arrived. They extracted the man from the car, placed him on a scoop stretcher, and whisked him into the ambulance. But the ambulance didn't leave, so neither did I or my fellow gawkers. I think our curiosity held us to the spot. In a few minutes, the man, middle-aged and clad in a navy blue suit, jumped from the ambulance. The crowd erupted in applause. He grinned and waved back at us like a politician. I smiled. In that moment, I felt a burst of happiness for the dumb luck of that day. What kept me a split second behind the SUV and out of the crash? What force had left that man and the driver of the other car unscathed? Maybe what we're looking so hard for in scenes of atrocity is evidence of God. When death brushes close, but doesn't grab us, we feel blessed. We want to know that even if suffering comes, it is not in vain. That our lives—even as they draw dangerously near to the horror—mean something. Photographer Walker Evans put it best, when he said, "Stare. It is the only way to educate your eye, and more. Stare, pry, listen, eavesdrop. Die knowing something. You are not here long."

THE BELLY OF DESIRE

Belly: The protruding abdomen of a pregnant woman

When I was five, I played the Pregnancy Game with the Slibny sisters, Julie and Melanie. We used my Cabbage Patch Kid, Tallulah, a coveted Christmas present in 1986, but one that turned out to be a disappointment because she was so ugly. Tallulah's hair—short loops of yellow yarn that haloed her head—looked like a helmet made of a hook rug. I hated her for that. Still, I played with her often enough that her soft limbs developed a patina of grime.

After dinner, while our parents sat around the table talking, we girls went to my bedroom to play. We fought over who got to stick Tallulah up her shirt, but I won because she was my doll.

"I'm going to have a baby!" I cried. Then as I had seen my mom do when she was pregnant with my little sister, I practiced Lamaze breathing—whooo, whooo, heeeeee.

Melanie, playing Nurse, had me lie down on the bed so she could stick my arm with a fake hypodermic—a retractable Bic pen. To us, babies came from bellies. We knew nothing of birth canals or uteruses, so every delivery necessitated a C-section. Doctor Julie reached in under my shirt with the scalpel—improvised from a plastic picnic knife with serrated edge—and

WHAT WILL OUTLAST ME?

swiped across the flesh of my abdomen, grasped Tallulah by her ankle, pulled her from under my Care Bears sweatshirt, and dangled her, triumphantly, above my head.

"You have a healthy baby girl," she said.

Once born, Tallulah was never fed, diapered, or rocked. My desire for child rearing began and ended with the drama of birth. The game was about being the center of attention.

2. Tummy: Slang for paunch

I got my tummy in the third grade. It came from eating too much fast food at the Chanticleer Drive-In. That was the year mom went back to work and stopped cooking, the year Dad lost the farm and we moved to a house in town. I was grieving my old home. As if by filling my tummy with French fries and hot fudge sundaes, I could fill a deeper emptiness.

Sometimes I sat naked on the toilet before bathing. I hunched over, grabbed the thick snake of fat that started at the side of my waist, pinched it away from my rib cage, and imagined ripping it off. When I reached the center of my abdomen, I had two handfuls of fatty flesh. My belly button disappeared into the fold. What remained looked like a giant, puckered mouth. I squeezed these blubber lips.

In the weeks leading up to my ninth birthday, I pored over Mom's Wilton-method cake decorating magazines, flipping through pictures of exquisite frosting designs. Buttercream frosting roses cascaded across the cake top with petals so delicate they looked like real flowers. Pastel-green leaves unfurled over paper-smooth fondant. The children pictured next to the birthday cakes fascinated me too. They were thin and smiled freely. I, on the other hand, sucked in my tummy anytime I thought someone might be looking, especially the eye of a camera. In most photos I wore a tense, pained look on my face, more grimace than smile.

I settled on a chocolate sheet cake trimmed with a shell-frosting border, a cascade of buttercream roses, and my name inscribed in pink frosting at the center. In the birthday snapshot, I wear a pink sweater stretched tight over my round tummy. I'm so caught up in the moment—seconds before I scoop one of those coveted roses off the cake and into my mouth—I forget to suck in my tummy. I smile, fat chipmunk cheeks framing my face. I look so happy knowing how the desired sugar will comfort me.

3. Midriff: Middle part of the body between chest and waist, often revealed to incite sexual appeal

The summer after third grade, my cousin Erin came to stay with my family. Having abandoned the Pregnancy Game, the Slibny girls and I taught Erin our new favorite: Dirty Dancing. Inspired by the 1987 film starring Patrick Swayze (which I watched on VHS until I'd memorized every line), we took turns dancing to the soundtrack. Still years from puberty, we couldn't see what was "dirty" about gyrating hips, but we got the love story. By the end of the film, Jennifer Gray's character, Baby Housman, won the love of Johnny, the sexy dance instructor. It inspired us to emulate her every move.

For Christmas that year, my mother had bought me the soundtrack, a vinyl LP. I played it on my Fisher-Price turntable. Using the song list on the album cover, we made elaborate dance lists, plotting out who danced each song.

WHAT WILL OUTLAST ME?

My song was Eric Carmen's hit, "Hungry Eyes." In the scene at the dance studio, Baby wears a pink bra and matching pink shorts. Johnny dances in front of her, and Penny (the dancer Baby will sub for once she learns the routine), dances behind, her hands on Baby's back and waist, guiding. In this composition, Baby's midriff is the focal point, centered in the screen. Her chiseled abs undulate under the slight twisting movement each dance step triggers. Sweat glistens on her skin.

In classic '80s-style montage, the film cuts to a series of dance practices, all revealing that delicious midriff, while Carmen croons about a feeling that will not subside. In the next cut, Baby wears a tight white crop top. Then we see only her torso, the black waistband of Jockey panties, and Johnny's hands at the side of her waist.

With the recent development of my own midriff, Baby's image was one to aspire to. Surely when I was older and had breasts, my torso would look like that. Baby gave me something to hope for while miserable at school and scared about how much my parents worried about money. Though I didn't feel sexual attraction yet at that age, the way Johnny held, hugged, and laughed with Baby in the movie filled me with a feeling that I couldn't describe.

4. Jelly Belly: A gourmet jellybean made in fifty-one flavors popular in America during the 1980s

When I was in fifth grade, every time Grandma B took me to the mall, she bought me jellybeans. Grandma had roughly the same measurements as the Laughing Buddha. She stood about five feet one, measured forty-five inches at the waist, and possessed wide, child-bearing hips that allowed her to have nine babies. Even without all that childbirth, she would have been bottom heavy. All the women on that side of the family have inherited her shape.

I had tried on twenty pairs of jeans at J. C. Penney, but the only pair that fit around my belly had hideous front pleats and an ugly acid wash. Grandma insisted on buying not one, but two, identical pairs of them since I couldn't get by with only one pair of school jeans. To my classmates, it'd look like I wore the same pair every day, making me look even poorer than we were. As we stood at the Jelly Belly store counter, I tried to forget the shopping bag hanging from my wrist.

Though you could choose separate flavors, I was too greedy, too worried about making the wrong choice and missing out. I ordered my usual—a ½ lb. assorted. I loved the brilliant colors—cactus-pad green, stop-light red, buttery-yellow, blue-indigo, all luminous like sea glass. I wanted them all. The cashier weighed the candy and shoveled it from bin to white-paper bag with a silver-handled scoop.

When I clutched the bag, the beans clinked like pebbles, each a promise of pleasure. I cupped my eye over the opening, so I saw a tunnel of white paper bag, and the end of it, a riot of bright-colored beans splendid as any kaleidoscope.

5. Muffin Top: Fatty flesh that spills over the waistline of pants or skirts because of tight clothing and/or excess body fat

When I was growing up, dressing up meant wearing No Nonsense Control-Top pantyhose, a modern replacement for the girdle, packaged in orange plastic envelopes. For church I wore dresses Mom had sewn from Simplicity patterns. On my

WHAT WILL OUTLAST ME?

body the finished garments never looked like the girls' dresses on the pattern envelope. The bodices were too big, the waists too tight across my stomach.

"Control tops will fix that," Mom said when the fabric puckered unflatteringly over my gut.

She helped me pull the nylons up my legs, pinching my skin in an attempt to grasp the flimsy material. The waistband dug into my flesh, but as soon as I pulled my dress over my head, the waistband rolled down, making a sausage. I pressed hard on my lower belly. Swathed in tight elastic, it took on the tautness of a basketball while forming a crest of muffin-soft flesh above the waistband.

By the time I started college, I'd stopped wearing control tops. They suffocated me. And I didn't need them anymore. The clothes off J.C. Penney's racks fit me fine. Though I wouldn't have described myself as thin, I kept my weight down by giving up junk food and by exercising.

I wore control top panty hose only once after leaving home, when my Mom and I went to a cousin's wedding and shared a hotel room for the weekend. As we were dressing, I snagged a runner through my pantyhose.

"I have a brand-new pair you can have," Mom said. She rummaged through her luggage and handed me the orange package, unchanged over the years. As I shimmed the tight pantyhose up my legs, she kept up a steady commentary on my appearance.

"*That* lipstick's awfully bright for your complexion," she noted as she fussed over her hair in the bathroom mirror. Her tone reminded me of Grandma B.

She nodded to my dress hanging from the towel rack and then to my Mary Jane flats. "Those shoes don't go with that hemline. Are they the only ones you brought?"

Standing there in my bra and pantyhose, I looked down at my belly. The pantyhose seam reminded me of a scar. I wanted to rip the nylons off my stomach. Instead, I helped my mother zip her dress. Like wearing pantyhose, this wedding was something to be endured.

Since middle school, I had compared myself to the bride, Melissa, and always came up short. She was thinner, prettier, and richer than me. For years I'd wanted to shuck off the fat around my midsection, but standing in that hotel room, a new desire came over me. I wished I were the bride.

6. Six-Pack: *A set of well-developed rectus abdominis*

My junior year of college, I dated a soldier. He had come back from Iraq hard and chiseled. As we lay in bed, I traced his six-pack with my tongue, then lightly kissed the six rippled muscles running from his pubic crest to his ribs. He was tan, lean, and smiled like a supermodel. My head told me, "He's sexy," but my body wasn't into it. I was so uncomfortable around him while naked, I could never climax. Once he ran his hands over my naked body but stopped suddenly at my stomach.

"What's wrong?" I asked.

"You're just so—soft," he said. "Not fat, but soft. You've got to do some sit ups or something." He grabbed at my belly and shook his hand like a dog wrestling a chew toy. I fought back tears when I thought about those hours

WHAT WILL OUTLAST ME?

of Pilates I had done when he was deployed, and still my body didn't make him—or me—happy.

When I got sick of faking orgasms, I broke up with the soldier. Even though I had done the dumping, I still felt like a failed husband catcher.

7. Solar Plexus: Nerves of the sympathetic system located at the pit of the stomach

    I found my solar plexus after breaking up with the soldier. I had enrolled in a Hatha yoga class at the university fitness center. Chakras, I learned, were the body's energy centers. The solar plexus chakra controlled my fear, anxiety, personal power, and transitions.

"Let your belly soften. On the inhale let it grow large. Grow round," the yogi instructed. To nurture calmness, he explained, you must breathe from the bottom of your belly.

We did Mountain Pose—or *Tadasana*—which didn't look like any yoga poses I'd imagined. We stood. Feet aligned parallel, hip width apart. Eyes closed. Arms hung with palms out. Energy floated through my body and tingled out my fingertips.

"You're like seaweed floating in the ocean," the yogi said. "Your bones can float around in your body." He told me to place my hand on my belly.

"Your belly is an air pillow," the yogi said. "You know when you order something from Amazon, and it comes with those little plastic pillows full of air?" I chuckled. He was right. Just like an air pillow, the flesh cupped in my hand was somehow firm and soft at the same time. I imagined a radiating yellow ball of energy revolving just under my solar plexus. My belly didn't feel fat. It was strong. Whole.

When the session was over, I stood as tall as a mountain, proud of my rugged crags and jagged outcroppings.

8. *Potbelly* [1]: *A swollen or protuberant stomach*

While dating Kent, the man I married, we went to midnight showings of cult-classic films in Midtown Omaha at the Dundee, a historic theater, the interior of which resembled a red velvet cake. Until I saw Quentin Tarantino's 1994 film *Pulp Fiction* there, I never thought a pot belly could be sexy. Fabienne (played by Maria de Medeiros) obsesses over blueberry pie and pot bellies. Her lover, Butch Coolidge (the boxer played by Bruce Willis) comes to her on the lam after killing his opponent in the ring.

She lolls on the bed of their dive-hotel room wearing a baggy T-shirt and a pair of cotton panties and says in a sexy French accent, "I was looking at myself in the mirror. I wish I had a pot. A potbelly. Potbellies are sexy."

"You should be happy, 'cause you do," Butch tells her.

She bristles, explaining that having a bit of tummy is not the same thing as a potbelly. Butch is perplexed and agitated, but she goes on.

"Potbellies make a man look either oafish or like a gorilla. But on a woman a potbelly is very sexy. The rest of you is normal. Normal face, normal legs, normal hips, normal ass, but with a big, perfectly round potbelly. If I had one, I'd wear a T-shirt two sizes too small to accentuate it."

"You think guys would find that attractive?" he asks.

WHAT WILL OUTLAST ME?

"I don't give a damn what men find attractive. It's unfortunate what we find pleasing to the touch and pleasing to the eye is seldom the same."

Potbelly [2]: Having a round, protruding shape

If you Google "potbelly," one of the hits will take you to photographs of the Guatemalan potbelly sculptures. Hundreds of them dot the Pacific slope and highlands, human figures portrayed as crude spheres with large, jutting guts. As if holding a ball, they cup their hands to their bellies. Some look fierce. Others tilt their heads back and stare into the sky with hollow, sunken eyes.

When I look at the Guatemalan potbelly sculptures in grainy black and white photos from archeological magazines, I imagine what it would be like to visit the sculptures, to walk along the wind-whipped coastal paradise, and to feel dwarfed by its twelve-ton body. Carved from basalt, a volcanic rock amalgam of large and small minerals, the sculptures' surface can be at once harsh and crude, smooth and fine. I want to run my hands over its rough velvet because it's one of the most beautiful things I've seen.

At first my attraction to these crude lumps puzzles me, until it dawns on me that until now my standards of beauty have had three sources: glossy magazines, the movies, and my mother. To all three I owe my shame at having a pronounced gut. For as long as I could remember, two contradictory and paradoxical desires—the wish for a flat midriff and the wish to be a mother—had tugged at me. I never questioned them, let alone their sources. Now I wondered if those urges were genuinely mine.

The potbelly statues were beautiful precisely because they shocked, and in doing so, broadened my sense of what is "acceptable." They're beautiful the way a Picasso painting is beautiful because it challenges staid notions of "beauty."

9. Baby Bump: The protruding abdomen of a visibly pregnant woman

After I turned thirty and had been married for five years, photos of pregnant bellies started crowding my Facebook. One by one, women I'd lost touch with over the years—the Slibny sisters, my cousins—appeared on my Facebook page, their bellies bloated by pregnancy. They pressed bellies up to sinks for bathroom mirror selfie shots. In professional portraits, they cupped their hands under their bellies and gazed lovingly down at their round protrusion.

When my younger sister got pregnant last year, it was the first time she ever beat me to a milestone. Putting careers first, my husband and I delayed starting our own family. The intense jealousy I felt over my sister's pregnancy—when I wasn't even trying to get pregnant—startled me. The latent longing for a baby suddenly sprang to life. It was like wanting Baby Housman's midriff all over again or envying Melissa when she was a bride (who, by the way, had just birthed her third beautiful baby).

The Christmas before my sister gave birth, she hired a photographer. She wanted to document her baby bump as it strained the elastic of her maternity jeans, and she wanted a family portrait too. One sunny day in early December I found myself with my mom and sister in a field with a photographer, who prompted us into posing.

WHAT WILL OUTLAST ME?

"Put your hands on her belly," she told us. My mom and I followed instructions. I'd never touched a pregnant belly before. I was shocked by how hard her bump felt, smooth as a wind-polished boulder, yet under that stony hardness a delicate fetus curled, floating in amniotic fluid—a future family member already beloved by my sister and her husband.

10. Rectus Abdominis: A long, flat, narrow muscle originating from the pubis to the seventh rib, forming part of the anterior abdominal wall

I was a year into a daily swimming and yoga regimen before I realized I had developed visible ab muscles. One evening I was packing for a business trip while my husband drank a beer and lounged on the bed. I tried on a new blouse, something slinky and tighter than anything else in my wardrobe.

"Does this blouse show too much belly?" I asked.

"You don't have belly to show."

I swiveled my hips in front of the mirror. He was right. For the first time in my life, I didn't look like I had a fat belly. After years fighting my flabby stomach with exercise, I had won. It took me a while to realize this because I had long ago stopped exercising to shrink my waist measurement. Somewhere along the line it became its own pleasurable routine, satisfying and satiating.

I took the blouse off, folded and packed it in my suitcase. I grabbed my husband's beer off the nightstand and stole a swig. My beer drinking days are numbered. I hope to get pregnant soon, and my relationship with my belly will change again. The women who posted Facebook photos of their baby bumps now tell me all about their tiger stripes.

11. Tiger Stripes: Stretch marks and scarring patterns remaining on a belly after pregnancy

I was twenty when a close friend had her first baby, and now almost fifteen years later I haven't tried to get pregnant yet, and she's still saving up for plastic surgery on her pregnancy-wrecked belly.

"Want to see something gross?" she said the last time I saw her. She lifted her shirt, revealing squishy, loose folds of skin that hung on her thin, petite frame between ribs and hips. The skin rippled with white scars.

Another friend, Jodi, sees her tiger stripes differently. She told me about her four-year-old daughter's curiosity. "When Elizabeth asked me what those marks were on my belly, I said, those are my tiger stripes. They're special because I got them when you were in my belly. You'll get tiger stripes too someday after you have a baby." Jodi smiles when she tells me how excited Elizabeth is to get stretch marks someday. I wonder if Elizabeth plays the Pregnancy Game with her dolls.

The year I turned thirty-five, my husband and I decided to have a baby. My pregnancy was fraught with worry about my baby's health and my health, but I also feared that pregnancy would wreck my body, that tiger stripes would feel shameful rather than empowering.

WHAT WILL OUTLAST ME?

12. Nigra Lingea: Latin for the "black line" that runs vertically along the abdomen of a pregnant woman due to increased hormones made by the placenta.

At twenty weeks the dark line—like a thick smug of eyeliner—etched across my abdomen. Like my heightened sense of smell and craving for potatoes, it was another oddity of pregnancy, indicating my body was under the influence of a new slurry of hormones beyond my control.

There was nothing to be done for the black line, but for stretch marks, I bought an expensive jar of "belly butter," an organic compound of shea butter and coconut oil the consistency of frosting that smelled like oranges. Every evening before bed, I slathered it on my basketball belly.

Surprisingly for the first time in my life, I loved the way my belly looked. It pleased me when people said, "You're all baby," noticing that except for my baby bump, I didn't look fatter. I bought maternity dresses made of clingy, stretchy fabric, which accentuated my pregnant belly. My sister texted me every few weeks during my pregnancy: "Send baby bump pics!" I sent her selfies taken in the bathroom mirror, revealing my bare abdomen. In those photos, you can see the nigra linea, how it looked like a seam, splitting me down the middle.

13. Diastasis Recti: separation of rectus abdominis muscles as a result of pregnancy.

I gave birth to a healthy son. When I got home from the hospital, still oozing lochia and wearing a gigantic maxi pad, I stepped on the bathroom scale, and it registered my pre-pregnancy weight. My belly, however, was not back to normal.

I knew that this was to be expected, as my uterus would take weeks to shrink, but at my six-week postpartum checkup, my abdomen was still a flabby mess. My OB had me lie back on the exam table and lift my shoulders in a crunch. She probed the center seam of my belly, and her fingers found it: a trough-like furrow where the ab muscles separated. She confirmed my fear. I had diastasis recti.

"Nothing will ever make it come back together the way it was before," she said, "except maybe surgery."

"But I've heard of exercises, physical therapy," I replied, wanting reassurance that I had the power to change my belly.

"Those are just snake-oil remedies."

A thorough search of medical journals revealed my doctor was right. I couldn't find a single study that confirmed exercise can heal split abdominal muscles.

14: Mummy Tummy: flabby, rounded belly of a woman who's given birth

When I was still pregnant, just a few months after my sister gave birth to her second child without an epidural, she sent me a video of a goat in labor. It made horrible, loud bellowing noises.

"What I sounded like in labor. You probably will too," she texted, punctuated by a laughing emoji.

I gave birth naturally because I wanted to see what my body could do without intervention. During labor, the pain felt like it would shatter me, and like my sister, and the goat, and countless women before me, I made loud vocalizations—high-pitched vowel sounds, like shrill yodeling. My sister was right. Instinct took over.

Four months after giving birth, despite the fact I could fit into my pre-pregnancy pants, my tummy was still an ugly, saggy thing. Then I remembered something else about goats. One summer during high school, I had worked on a goat farm. There I'd learned that you could tell if a goat had ever given birth just by the curve of her belly. As I struggled to return my belly to its former firmness, I wondered, why should it be different for humans? But the better question is: why do we expect a woman to look like something she isn't? It seemed unrealistic given the gravitas of childbirth that the body wouldn't be irrevocably altered.

One predictable change motherhood brought was a lack of free time. Of the scant hours a week I carved for myself, I managed to sneak in swimming and yoga but realized I would never have enough time for exercise or enough money for surgery to chisel the belly I wanted. I have wasted thousands of hours on my belly: worrying about it, finding clothes to conceal it, trying diets that promise to flatten it. Maybe I will never feel totally at peace with my tummy, but at least when I think of all my body has done, I feel good.

Every morning now I nurse my son skin-to-skin. He nestles in. My mummy tummy makes a soft shelf for him to lay on. He is smooth and warm. Intoxicating pheromones waft from the top of his head. I breathe in his smell. He makes small suckling sounds. His tiny, splayed hand rests on my breast. What a miracle that this delicate, beautiful creature grew inside my abdomen. And I wonder, why should I want to look like he hadn't?

SO MANY WAYS

There are so many ways a baby can die that even in my sleep, I imagine it: I am smothering my newborn baby. Clutching his delicate, fontanelle-cratered skull under my arm, I draw his small mouth and nose into the suffocating crevasse of my armpit. As I break the surface of dreamland, my baby's skull morphs into a wadded-up quilt. I am panting, drenched in sweat.

My son, Stanley, sleeps in his bassinette an arm's length from my bed. I roll over to look at him. He's beginning to rouse. He sputters and grunts. It must have been this noise that woke me. It's only been five days since he was born, but ever since the night I gave birth, I've been wired. A storm surge of hormones is revving me up. Everything thrums with anxiety. My sleep is shallow and fraught with disturbing dreams. My waking hours are consumed with worry about my baby and fear that something will harm him.

There are so many ways a baby can die.

Yesterday, I had my first scare. My milk had just come in, and Stanley latched well and sucked vigorously. He nursed and nursed but still seemed desperately hungry. I suspected something was wrong when he wasn't pooping yet, his diapers still smeared with tarry black meconium. If he wasn't nursing,

WHAT WILL OUTLAST ME?

he cried, so we'd spent the first six hours of the day nursing in bed, his head tucked next to my bicep. When his urine turned a rusty dark red called brick dust that smelled like rancid peanut butter, I panicked. I knew from the childbirth classes Kent and I had taken that brick dust was bad—a sign of dehydration.

"I don't think he's getting enough milk," I said.

"What do we do?" Kent asked.

"I don't know." I didn't want to feed my precious new baby a powder that had been produced in a factory with corn syrup solids and chemicals, yet I was terrified that if I didn't, he'd—I couldn't even finish that sentence.

In desperation, I told Kent, "I think we should give him some formula." He immediately got on it, rummaging through the nursery closet to find the free sample of formula the hospital sent home with us, the one I'd almost refused with derision because we were going to breastfeed exclusively, thank-you-very-much.

He mixed one ounce of formula in a bottle. We gave it to Stanley, and ten minutes later, he was a different baby. Calm. His fists finally relaxed into tiny starfishes of splayed fingers. Then a few hours later, a real baby poop—yellow and seedy like whole grain mustard—just as it should be. I knew I wasn't producing enough milk, and it devastated me. But I also knew we'd headed off a crisis. What if we hadn't known something was wrong?

There are so many ways a baby can die.

By whooping cough, influenza, pneumonia, RSV, measles, mumps, or rubella, or any of those other childhood diseases he can't be vaccinated for until he's six months old but can be spread by some anti-vaxxer. By a gastrointestinal virus from contaminated formula, or an unwashed hand, and then by the subsequent diarrhea leading to deadly dehydration. By blunt force trauma to the head if I tripped and dropped the baby, and he smashed into a brick retaining wall like in that short story by Lorrie Moore. If something heavy accidently fell on him, a toppled piece of furniture, a lamp, a large book. Strangulation by venetian blind cord, by the straps of his car seat malfunctioning, by the ribbon that holds his paci, by the cords that tighten his hood. By drowning in a bathtub, in as little as an inch of water. By smothering, perhaps by one of our lazy, but malicious housecats. By a potentially faulty crib mattress. By a spider bite. By West Nile from a mosquito bite. By typhus from a flea bite. By choking on a piece of food. By inhaling a piece of latex from a popped balloon. By ways and means I haven't imagined, couldn't possibly imagine, but could kill him nonetheless.

There are so many ways a baby can die.

Even before he was born, I feared sudden infant death syndrome. When I was seventeen, I worked the snack counter at a Mom and Pop bowling alley. The owner, Tami, gave birth to her second daughter a few weeks after I started the job, and a few weeks after that, her baby died of SIDS. It shocked me how a baby could mysteriously die, just stop breathing for no reason at all. Now that I'd given birth to my own baby, every memory I ever had of a baby dying—be it real or fiction—flooded my thoughts.

When my baby was born, I made sure to do all the right things. Absolutely no co-sleeping—if there was a lesson to be learned from my nightmare, it was that I might accidentally kill

WHAT WILL OUTLAST ME?

this tiny human. No loose clothing. Form-fitting, footed pajamas only. No swaddling, lest he rollover and become trapped face down. No blankets or stuffed toys. A rigorously safety-tested crib and crib mattress with tight fitting sheets. The baby books also instructed to keep the room cool and keep a fan running. For this, Kent had dug a small table fan out of the closet. Years ago, he had stuck a Superman sticker to the center of the grate. At every nap and before bed, I clicked the small fan on. When I prayed for my baby's safety, yes, I implored God, but I was tempted to ask any benevolent supernatural force—even Superman—to protect my baby, if it would work.

Fear, I learned, breeds superstitions.

During my eight-week maternity leave, my world shrunk to Kent, me, and Baby Stanley—an isolated triad, hunkered down in our home away from the relentless heat of South Texas summer. The few times I escaped the house to go to a postnatal yoga class, or get groceries at the H.E.B., I'd pass a billboard: Never, ever, shake a baby. Seeing the ten-foot-tall baby, mouth wide and wailing, chilled me. The PSA's admonishment made me doubt my ability to keep my son safe. Would I suddenly snap and shake Stanley if he wouldn't stop crying? I thought about how shaking a baby causes bleeding on the brain, seizures, and death. If there needs to be a billboard here as a reminder, then parents do this. Often. I reasoned. What if was one of them? I felt my heart pound under my sternum.

There are so many ways a baby can die.

I was on high alert all the time during those first two months. The anxiety came in waves, and my survival strategy was just to keep going, to fight against it. I had been warned about postpartum depression, to let my husband or my doctor know if I had thoughts about harming my baby or harming myself, but this wasn't it. What I was experiencing was the opposite of that—I had to be ever vigilant, lest some harm came to Stanley. As his mother, it was up to me to protect him from the world.

I knew exercise supported my mental health. Before I'd gotten pregnant, I managed my anxiety with intense cardio workouts. I had swum laps up until four days before I gave birth. Slicing through the water, churning all my limbs in a pattern synchronized with breath, making my heart pound and lungs expand, and getting an endorphin hit was the most effective thing I knew to wring anxiety out of my body. But after having a baby, swimming was prohibited for at least seven weeks. The only exercise available to me was walking.

We had a jogging stroller with giant spoked bicycle wheels. The baby's infant carrier snapped into it like an old-fashioned pram with a canopy. Early in the morning, after I nursed Stanley, I strapped him into his carrier. We set out at sunrise.

Our neighborhood in Corpus Christi was an older one. Like ours, most of the houses were built in the 1950s on thick but unstable clay soil. During the rainy hurricane seasons, the earth swelled and thickened like a brackish pudding, and during *la canicula*, the dog days of summer, the soil parched and split. The grass in our backyard had long turned brown in the scorching heat, and under it the ground broke itself into jagged pieces with fault lines two inches wide in places, a scaled down model of plate tectonics. Because of the unstable swing of the soil, the sidewalks in most of our neighborhood buckled like the rubble in an earthquake. In the beginning, it felt fraught navigating the jagged sidewalks. I hadn't realized before how

WHAT WILL OUTLAST ME?

precarious an infant's head is, such a heavy skull on a floppy neck that has no muscle control. The stroller's tires strained then bounced over bumps. Stanley's head jerked and bobbed. I held my breath, clinching my body unconsciously as his tiny body jostled. I learned to follow a route on the streets one block east of our house, where sidewalks were smoother. At this hour, our neighborhood was silent, except for the mourning doves. Live oak trees above us made a canopy of shade.

Even in this relatively peaceful setting, the very air felt violent. Though the sun was just beginning to rise, the weather felt like a sauna—80 degrees and 80 percent humidity. Everything under my shirt dampened. My nipples leaked breastmilk and sweat beaded up in my cleavage. Still, I walked, hoping for some relief from my worry. As my legs strode through the hot, thick air, my heart revved with a tightness that had more to do with anxiety than exertion. It was so hot that it was easy to imagine the catastrophic effects of global warming. I looked across Alameda Street—the busy throughway that creates the boundary of our neighborhood—and a couple of blocks beyond that I saw how the horizon drops into the Bay of Corpus Christi, and beyond that, the Gulf of Mexico. As a Midwestern native, I'm still unaccustomed to being so close to the shore. I imagined how the world will be decimated by the time Stanley is an adult. Artic ice caps gone. Polar bears extinct. Coral reefs dead. Our house swept away by the rising ocean. In a few decades isn't it possible, I thought, that everything around me, houses, palm trees, streets, will be underwater, lost like Atlantis?

I kept a constant vigil on Stanley, so I noticed every detail of how his breath moved his tiny chest up and down. I watched his skin—fresh and smooth—yet chameleon-like. It changed in response to the environment and to his mood. The heat mottled his skin in unpredictable red patches on the insides of his elbows. One eyelid turned crimson. He had a birthmark on the back of his neck. The baby books called them stork bites—a moniker that connotes both the mythical and violent quality of birth. Though I knew the birth mark was harmless and would eventually fade, the sight of it—a red slash under his skin that darkens when he cries—unnerved me. It was too much like a contusion.

There are so many ways a baby can die.

We turned the corner to weave back toward our house. We were close to Driscoll Children's Hospital, which is only six blocks from home. When I couldn't sleep at night, and I imagined an emergency with Stanley—a sudden fever spike, convulsions, or an injury—in my mind I traced the quickest route to the hospital, behind the H.E.B. grocery, past the Whataburger, and through the automatic sliding doors of the emergency ward with a whoosh. The Children's Hospital has an electronic billboard near the Life Flight helicopter pad. It always upset me. Often it was the promotion of their child oncology ward, which flashed photographs of bald pediatric leukemia patients that brought me to tears, but on this particular day, there was a new PSA: Look before you lock! Never leave a child in alone in a car.

Who would leave their child in a car? In this heat? I imagined some strung-out drug addict, a poster parent for Child Protective Services, someone named Snake with facial tattoos. A parent that embodies evil. I would never do something like that, I think with relief.

WHAT WILL OUTLAST ME?

Stanley had fallen asleep during our walk. The hum of the garage door wasn't loud enough to rouse him, so I docked the stroller in the garage, unsnapped his carrier from the stroller, and lugged him into the kitchen. The air was gloriously conditioned to a dehumidified seventy-five degrees, which felt as cool as the inside of a refrigerator on my heat-laden skin. I set Stanley, still sleeping safely in his carrier, on the kitchen floor by the table. I rummaged through the fridge, ravenous for breakfast.

I was spooning refrigerator oatmeal sprinkled with Brewer's yeast (which supposedly would increase my milk supply) into my mouth and scrolling through my Facebook feed, when I saw it. "Fatal Distraction," the headline read. "Forgetting a Child in the Backseat of a Car Is a Horrifying Mistake. Is It a Crime?" I clicked through and began to read.

I am the type of person who, when fearful of something, wants to know the worst-case scenario, so I can anticipate and brace myself for it. The next worst thing that can happen, I reasoned, is being caught off guard by the worst thing happening. This is why I knew, like a litany, so many ways a baby can die.

The article stripped away any hubris I had about being a good mom. It slashed through my notion that only grossly negligent parents leave their children in a car to die. Leaving a child alone in a car to die could happen to anyone. A voice in my head pounded, "It could happen to you."

These lapses of memory aren't related to drug abuse or mental illness; they are a common brain-function mechanism combined with the bad luck of situation and timing. The basal ganglia region of the brain functions as the mind's autopilot, while the hippocampus is responsible for short-term memory. In all the instances in which a child had been killed from being forgotten in the car, the same factors kept showing up: "stress, emotion, lack of sleep, and change in routine." These factors cause the memory circuits in the hippocampus to get overwritten so the memory of the child in the backseat completely disappears as the basal ganglia takes over.

I already didn't trust my brain, the way it tricked me into thinking that I was smothering Stanley in my sleep. The way it wouldn't turn off the incessant chatter narrating every worry I had about Stanley, about the world, and about the future. I didn't like the way my rational brain seemed to be shorted out, and in its place, there was a new emotional switchboard overtaking my system. Alarmingly, anything could set off fat, sloppy tears. There was no telling what would start a crying jag—and the tears were of every ilk—joy, rage, or sorrow. I cried when Stanley looked me soberly in the eye one morning with the sage wisdom of the universe only newborns seem to possess from having just arrived in the world. I cried when Kent overcooked the chicken piccata for dinner. I cried when our friends, Robert and Sam, brought over a beautifully inscribed children's storybook as a baby gift. I cried when I saw the wrecked saggy skin of my deflated belly. I cried one morning on our walk when an emaciated stray mother-dog with sagging teats crossed our path. I cried when we watched a baseball game on TV and the Ford truck ads were too sentimental because it was almost Father's Day. I cried when I read in the local newspaper about *la canicula* because now I knew why the air around me felt evil and threatening. According to local columnist Nick Jimenez, canicular days are mid-July to mid-

WHAT WILL OUTLAST ME?

August, signaling the most brutal heatwave of the year. They end when Sirius, the bright Dog Star, returns to the night sky. In Mexican folklore, strange things happen during canicula. Parents are urged to keep their children out of the sun. Meat rots more readily. Infection and illness are more dangerous, so surgery should be avoided during la canicula as well. I couldn't help but think—*during canicula, babies who are forgotten in cars die more quickly.*

There are so many ways a baby can die.

Now I had just learned of another one: death by hyperthermia, fatal heatstroke. When this happens, the baby's body turns a reddish-purple color, but the abdomen takes on a green discoloration. The internal organs could reach a temperature of over 108 degrees. Heart and liver and stomach melt, and then autolysis, which caused the same distention I saw in roadkill carcasses, just like the cat that had been hit by a car on Harrison Street, which I'd seen during our stroller walk the morning before, bloated in the unrelenting heat, and which also made me cry.

A few mornings later, I received the first omen that a disaster was going to strike. Like most bad news I received, it came from Facebook. A colleague had posted a spaghetti model of a tropical depression forming East of Barbados. I eyed it with curiosity, scrolling through my phone while Stanley nursed. This was only my third summer as a coastal dweller. I knew nothing about hurricanes. The next day Kent monitored the storm obsessively, hitting the refresh button on weather newsfeeds on his laptop over and over. When I came into the living room after getting Stanley down for bed, I found Kent hunched over his computer that sat on the coffee table. Tension radiated off his body.

"How worried should we be?" I asked.

"I don't know yet."

"Do we need to evacuate?"

"I don't know," he snapped. "Let me show you what concerns me."

He pulled up another spaghetti model map, but unlike the previous one, this showed red tendrils looping up from the Gulf and landing over Corpus Christi, dead center, and then orange strings on the outskirts—in places like Ingleside, Port Aransas, and Rockport.

"How accurate are they?"

"I don't know. They say it could be a category four hurricane."

"What should we do?"

"I don't know."

The day before, I'd gone to Walmart to stock up on supplies. I'd read up on hurricane preparedness on my phone while nursing Stanley. FEMA's guidelines said having food and water for a minimum of three days was a necessity. At Walmart, it looked as if the disaster had already hit. I picked my way through bare shelves, scooping up the last few cans of tuna and baked beans. The store buzzed with the worried energy of its shoppers. They were completely sold out of water—and I had texted Kent—begging him to get some on the way home. He came home with several blocky three-gallon jugs.

"I'm going to try to get some sleep." I was exhausted and knew I should follow that adage: "sleep when the baby sleeps."

WHAT WILL OUTLAST ME?

I woke at two a.m., breasts full and aching. I had perfected pumping in bed while in a near half-slumber without turning on any lights. I connected the breast pump and after a few minutes of its mechanical pulsing, it screeched and went silent. I pushed the power button. Nothing. I turned on the bedside lamp, squinting in the sudden glare. The thing was dead. Milk still filled my breasts. Do I dare wake up Stanley to nurse? When I walked into the living room, Kent was still up, hunched over his laptop.

"My breast pump just died."

"What?"

"It just conked out. What are you looking at?"

He slid his laptop into my slight line. It was another spaghetti model—this one projected straight toward us with even fewer possible variations.

"We have to evacuate," he said. "We just can't take the risk if it's a direct hit."

We hatched a plan. Kent had already called our friends in Austin, Paul and Ben, to see if we could stay with them. They lived in a big house with a guest room we were welcome to use. We'd try to get a good night's sleep and then spend the next morning packing up, and we'd get on the road by lunchtime. Nervous energy made my limbs feel icy, though my breasts burned hot with milk. I decided to rouse Stanley to nurse. I scooped him from his crib and nestled in with him on the rocking chair. He latched on without opening his eyes. Occasionally, he made contented sighs like a kitten. The warmth of his body, the heavy languor of his sleep-relaxed limbs calmed me.

"Don't worry about a thing," I whispered. "Tomorrow we're going on an adventure."

Just before we evacuated, I took one last look around our living room. I imagined it flooded, a foot of murky water covering the floor—Stanley's plastic teething toys floating like baby ducks, the coffee table bobbing like a dingy. Material things felt inconsequential. I looked at Stanley strapped in his carrier.

"Are you ready to go?"

He kicked his fat little thighs in response. Kent scooped up Stanley. As I locked the front door, I felt how small our house was compared to the power of a category four hurricane, how big the forces that could harm and kill were, but also how lucky we were that we had a safe place to go, and an easy way to get there. It also seemed surreal. Being from the Midwest, I wasn't used to the long timelines of hurricanes. The most common natural disaster I'd faced growing up were tornados, which were no less terrifying, but at least were quick. Sirens would sound, we'd take cover in a basement, and wait it out for an hour, and then it'd be over.

As Kent merged us onto I-37, it felt like we were going on a road trip. A weekend getaway. Though the air was hot and heavy with humidity, the sun still shone, and the violent storm gathering strength in the Gulf seemed a distant reality. Stanley fell asleep in his car seat.

"What are you thinking about?" I asked Kent.

"Maybe we should have taken the time to board up all our windows. What are you thinking about?"

WHAT WILL OUTLAST ME?

I told him about the article about babies dying after being forgotten in hot cars. I realized how good it felt to tell someone else my fear, no matter how irrational.

"That'd never happen to us," he said.

"But that's the thing, it could. That's the whole point of the article. Sometimes all the holes of the Swiss cheese line up."

"What are you talking about?"

I explained about the Swiss cheese model of safeguards. Say you forget the baby in the car, but daycare calls, wondering why you didn't drop off the baby. That's a slice of cheese—you've been reminded of the baby before it dies of heatstroke. But the holes in Swiss cheese represent a safety check that fails. Say daycare calls, but you miss the call because your cellphone's battery just died, then you've fallen through a hole. When catastrophe strikes, it's because all the holes in each layer of Swiss cheese line up.

"You think about things like this too much."

"I know. I can't help it."

At Paul and Ben's house, surprisingly, I felt calm. Stanley was safe. Tending to his simple newborn needs—the predictable pattern of feeding, diapering, rocking to sleep, and bathing—preoccupied me enough to shut out darker worries. For days, we lived in a state of suspension, not knowing if our house was going to be leveled by the gale winds or flooded by the massive rains.

The night the hurricane hit, we stayed up late watching the Weather Channel reports. Hurricane Harvey made landfall thirty miles north of where we lived, and the next morning, our neighbor called to report that he saw no damage on our property. Even the rickety privacy fence around the backyard had stood strong.

Ben suggested we go out to dinner to celebrate our good fortune. Paul, who was a medical doctor, offered to babysit that night. I found it comforting that Paul's training meant he could attend to any medical emergency. I took him up on his offer, and for the first time since he was born, left Stanley.

At the restaurant we ate sous vide fish and Thai meatballs, and without the baby nearby, I began to feel like my old self. The immediate crisis was over, and through random chance, we'd been spared. We did what we could to secure our safety, but as I popped another spicy meatball in my mouth, I knew that our vigilance could only go so far. Sometimes bad, devastating things happen, and it's no one's fault. Though I—along with Kent—am responsible for my son's safety and wellbeing, I realized we couldn't possibly be perfect in this parenting endeavor. Shouldering that type of responsibility without any mistakes or missteps was impossible. Not because we weren't capable parents, but because too many other forces were beyond our control.

We returned home a week later, having waited until our electrical power was restored after the storm. Aside from the dead-flesh smell of rotten food in our refrigerator, everything was just as we left it. I thought about those signs hung in workplaces on chalkboards with a number written in: ___ days without an accident. We'd had Stanley for fifty-six days now, and they had been fifty-six days without an accident. The fear something terrible will happen to him or that he will die will

WHAT WILL OUTLAST ME?

never go away. I will always carry it along with the love I have for him. As the number of days without an accident grew (we hit 180 and then 365, and soon we will hit 730), I realized I'd become accustomed to the fear. It was one of the layers of Swiss cheese, perhaps even the one that contained the fewest holes, and I began to trust in the fear. It was the mechanism that kept Stanley safe, that kept him alive and well.

WHAT CANNOT BE HELPED

We arrived at the Coastal Bend Surgical Center at dawn. In the reception area, half a dozen pajama-clad babies and toddlers sat drowsy-eyed on the laps of their parents. Because the young patients were fasting, food and drink wasn't allowed, so Kent had reluctantly left his coffee thermos in the car. I could see how tired he was as he carried our nineteen-month-old son. We'd brought Stanley to have a myringotomy. A surgeon would insert tubes into his eardrum to drain the perpetual buildup of mucus in his inner ear.

We'd known for over a year now that this day would come, that finally, it would make less sense to have Stanley suffer from an ear infection every four weeks, than to avoid a relatively simple and safe procedure. When it was clear at his eighteen-month checkup that he had significant hearing loss and speech delays, we finally made the appointment with the specialist, Dr. Weiss. I trusted Dr. Weiss because he was the ENT surgeon who'd removed my thyroid after I was diagnosed with cancer.

As I waited for them to call my name to fill out paperwork, I sized up the other kids. The nurse had said that the surgery schedule was determined by age. I saw a baby girl in pink floral footed pajamas who must have been the first in line, as she looked only six months old—too young to even walk. I saw two

WHAT WILL OUTLAST ME?

other boys that were obviously younger than Stanley, and then another that looked exactly his age.

Stanley fussed and squirmed in Kent's lap until he let him down. Stanley wanted to explore and make friends. He walked right up to a Black boy and looked him straight in the eyes with friendly curiosity, and the other boy did the same. They stood with the same stature of all toddlers: thin arms and legs, big heads, rounded pot bellies. Stanley's fine, blond hair stood up in tousled snarls, the black boy's tight curls made a halo.

"For Harper!" the check-in nurse yelled, breaking the quiet.

"That's us," the boy's mom said, as she took Harper by the hand and walked across the room to the check-in desk.

There was nothing to do in the waiting room but observe, so I watched Harper's mom. She looked young, but not too young. She wore yoga pants and a T-shirt. Her hair was done up in sleek braids. The nurse went on about a payment plan.

"So you want the payments deducted monthly, on the fifteenth?" she asked. I felt guilty that her financial situation was being disclosed to the whole waiting room, that the nurse didn't have any discretion. Harper began to fuss.

"No whining," she said firmly. He immediately stopped. "Use your words." He mumbled something I didn't catch, and she let him down off her lap. The comparisons came quickly, in a stream that I couldn't turn off. *She's a much better mom than I am. She's good with discipline. He listens. I'm too soft with Stanley. I let him do whatever he wants.* Harper walked over to where Stanley stood near my chair. He wore a pair of pajamas with red fire trucks on them. Stanley's pajamas had blue cars.

"Truck," Stanley said, pointing at the fabric's print.

"That's right! Truck!" I parroted. Truck and ball were the only two words Stanley used. He should have had at least a dozen words by now.

When Harper's mom finished signing paperwork, she sat down on the row of chairs behind us, and I twisted my body over the back of my chair.

"How old is he?" I asked.

"Eighteen months."

He's before us on the schedule then.

"Are you making a friend?" I asked the toddlers, but they were locked in a stare down. Harper turned away from Stanley and back to his mom, where she thumbed through a copy of *Arguing about Literature*. I knew that textbook cover because I used it for the online class I taught at the local community college.

"Are you taking English 1302?" I asked.

"Yeah. I thought I'd read my homework now, and then do the rest this afternoon when he's groggy from the operation."

"I teach English at Del Mar. I use that same textbook. What are you reading?"

"'As I Stand Here Ironing.'"

"That's a good one. Tillie Olsen has a good perspective on motherhood."

"When I heard what it was about, I said to myself, that's a good mom one."

"It is."

WHAT WILL OUTLAST ME?

The nurse opened the door to the pre-op area and called Harper's name. I'd read Tillie Olsen's years ago as an undergrad. I recalled being so angry at the narrator-mother for not being more involved in her child's life. Now though, I thought about how that mother had tried to do everything right. She nursed her daughter, Emily, because "they" felt that was important nowadays. She nursed her "with all the fierce rigidity of first motherhood...like all the books said." When Emily was two, she was "old enough for nursery school they said," so she went. Throughout the first part of the story, there's the refrain *they said*, and now with Stanley, I heard those same voices echoing. I imagine these were the same voices Harper's mom hears too.

They said Stanley has hearing loss. They said he has language delays. They said the language delays could lead to delayed literacy, to a child who starts school behind the learning curve. They said the benefits of a myringotomy were so great, and the risks so few, they implied I'd be ignorant not to give this benefit to my child. They said there was only a tiny, infinitesimal risk that there would be a complication from anesthesia.

Like Olsen's narrator, I did what they told us. They—the pediatricians, the ENT specialists, the other parents, the Web MD articles I Googled on my phone—all said have the surgery.

There's another tension in Olsen's story, though. The narrator struggles against her own needs and responsibilities beyond Emily, which she tries to balance against Emily's needs, but mostly, she fails. Like Olsen's unnamed narrator, Harper's mom and I struggled to have enough time to devote to our children. There was my fulltime teaching job and my writing career. Her fulltime academic load. With such time deficits, our sleep was usually the first thing to suffer, so that was another motivation to have the surgery. When the fluid clogs our sons' ears, it's painful, especially to lay down, and so they wake, wailing at 2 a.m., 3 a.m., 4 a.m. Did we sign our sons up for surgery selfishly, hoping that without the earaches, we'd all finally get some sleep?

When the nurse called, "For Stanley," I went to the intake desk while Kent entertained Stanley. He got Thomas the Train out of the diaper bag, and Stanley ran it up and down the arms of the chair. She handed me an iPad to check forms, verify insurance, sign for my acknowledgement of risks.

A laminated sheet on the desk entitled "Risks of Anesthesia to Children," enumerated the perils Stanley faced this morning. I'd done the research. One small study had concluded anesthesia exposure in children under the age of 2 were more like to have language and speech difficulties (ironic because that is what we were trying to avoid by having he surgery in the first place). A study of Danish birth cohorts cancelled out those findings and showed that by age sixteen there was no discernable cognitive or academic difference between children that had had anesthesia and those that hadn't.

The laminated sheet on the desk said, "The cognitive risks of anesthesia in pediatric patients are unknown. We need more studies to fully understand the effects of anesthesia on developing brains, hearts, and lungs."

I hesitated for a second, and then I signed the form.

Was I just like Olsen's narrator, I wondered, trusting what "they" say?

WHAT WILL OUTLAST ME?

The nurse finally called Stanley's name and ushered us into the pre-op area. Like a hospital emergency room, hospital beds stood in facing rows, separated only by curtains. Across the room we saw the post-op area. We sat in our curtained cubicle, waiting for the nurse to take Stanley's vitals, and then for him to be taken into the operating room.

Before we saw it, we heard the commotion—the worst crying I've ever heard. Not a wail so much as a choking gurgle.

"Harper, it's okay. Harper, stay with me." I heard someone say, and I saw Harper being wheeled on a stretcher. They stopped at the curtained cubicle across from us. Nurses and doctors rushed his bed from all directions. A machine beeped— a plaintive alarm—and my heart pounded faster, as if to match its terrifying rhythm.

Stanley, fixated on trying to punch the buttons on the blood pressure machine, didn't notice Harper's emergency at all.

From the huddle around Harper's bed, I heard the raspy sputter of a suction tube—like the kind you hear at the dentist. The crowd of nurses cleared. Harper's legs kicked. The fire engines on his pajama pants pumped up and down as he thrashed, fighting against the tube at his nose and mouth.

The doctor suctioned out the mucus so he could breathe. A retching sound. The suction sound stopped, and Harper's cry pierced the air. No longer clogged with snot and fluid, his cry made a sad bleating.

The doctor picked Harper up and handed him to his mother. She buried her face in the crook of his tiny neck.

"Oh my God, that was scary," I whispered to Kent.

"What?"

"He almost stopped breathing."

Kent shrugged and scooped Stanley up because he tried to run away. Kent held him, close, trying to contain his excessive energy. I felt angry that Kent underreacted. He seemed too calm and nonchalant. How did he not notice that Harper almost—well maybe I had overreacted—but how could I really know how bad it had been? I couldn't stop the cold seep of fear. *What if the same thing happened to Stanley?*

Harper kept crying, but softer now, a hoarse rasp. I was relieved that I could hear air reaching his lungs, but his crying jangled my nerves.

It was not too late to tell them, "No thanks, we've changed our mind." Was it really worth the risk? Wouldn't the fluid build-up behind his ears go away, eventually? Why risk it?

The anesthesiologist walked into our cubicle. I instantly hated him for his arrogant swagger. His body language seemed to say, what just happened to Harper, a few feet away from us, was no big deal. He didn't even look up at us when he asked the perfunctory questions and noted them in Stanley's chart.

"Has he ever been under anesthesia before? Do his parents have a history of having complications with anesthesia?"

I thought back to the bright yellow bile I vomited after I came to from my thyroidectomy. "Yes," I said, and he looked up at me for the first time as I explained how I'd thrown up after anesthesia when I'd had a thyroidectomy.

I imagined Stanley vomiting and choking too. The sinister suction tube, the violent thrashing. As if he could read my mind, the anesthesiologist said, "That's very uncommon, you

WHAT WILL OUTLAST ME?

know. What happened over there. He had a mild breathing problem. Mucus built up, briefly, and blocked his airways. I don't suspect it will happen with your son."

"But it's possible," I said.

He sighed. "Yes, it's possible, but rare."

I thought about Tillie Olsen's narrator, her resignation. My choice seemed to evaporate. It would be ridiculous not to have the surgery. I'd be judged as hysterical if I said no now. The nurse came to take Stanley to the operating room. The automatic door to the OR whooshed open. In a falsely bright voice, the nurse said, "All ready to go?" She held out her hand. He took it. He marched purposefully into the OR without looking back.

*

We were whisked back into the waiting room. The emotional contrast of people seemed more pronounced now. The nurses were bored by the routine, while the parents were fraught. The parents of the six-month-old baby, sat clutching each other's hands in white-knuckled worry. I wondered if they prayed. Until I saw their hands clasped together like that, the thought hadn't occurred to me.

Six months ago, Dr. Weiss had performed my thyroidectomy, not at a surgical center, but at a Catholic hospital. There we could not escape the religious iconography. Crucifixes hung in every room. Right before my surgery, as I sat in the pre-op area—in a surgical gown and with an IV line piercing the back of my hand—I nursed Stanley. I wanted him to nurse as much as he could before the anesthesia and pain killers tainted my milk, making it unsafe for him to drink.

While Stanley sucked away in pure contentment, the hospital chaplain knocked.

"Yes?"

"Would you like prayer?" he started to say, but then when he stuck his head through the door and saw my breast, he fumbled, embarrassed. "I'll come back later." He never came back.

*

We waited for Stanley. Why didn't I pray before? Why didn't I have an urge to pray now? Maybe it's because the moment the OR door closed behind Stanley, I had already surrendered my control over the situation. Sometimes it seemed that prayer was a means to wrest control over the situation, and it felt less like trusting and more like begging for my selfish wants. I found it hard to imagine God controlling every single event in the world as if pushing buttons on a cosmic videogame. I also found it difficult to know if prayer was effective. It wasn't like there was a control group to compare outcomes to. Had Harper's mother prayed? Was his breathing trauma an answer? If Stanley came out okay, was that God, luck, or a skilled surgeon? How would I ever know if the hearing improvements the surgery would supposedly bring outweighed the determents of the anesthesia? Under so much uncertainty, my reaction—as I reached for my phone to mindlessly scroll social media—was inertia.

After what seemed like an impossibly short few minutes, Kent and I were jolted from our smartphones when Dr. Weiss walked up. He pulled his surgical mask down under his chin to

WHAT WILL OUTLAST ME?

talk with us. I trusted Dr. Weiss. He was earnest. He never had broken eye contact with me, even when I asked him difficult questions.

"Surgery went well. No complications. You'll see an almost immediate difference in his hearing." He shook our hands and disappeared back into the pre-op area.

We heard Stanley's cry even before the nurse called out, "For Stanley's parents." I could have picked that cry out from anywhere. Suddenly I was scooping him from the hospital bed, and when he registered it was me, his eyes rolled back in his head, his body went limp and rubbery against my chest. My stomach dipped in anxiety for a moment, and then he regained consciousness.

I sat on the molded plastic chair and lifted my shirt to offer my breast. I had listened to what they, from the La Leche League, said about the benefits of long-term breastfeeding. Only after Stanley latched and started nursing vigorously did I begin to relax.

"You're free to go," the nurse said, standing across the bed from us.

"I'd like to nurse him until he's done."

Stanley was groggy, but he seemed unharmed from the ten-minute procedure.

"You did so good," I told him. I stroked the hair across his forehead, relieved that he smelled the same. His blue eyes fluttered to meet mine for an instant and then closed again.

"You're free to go now," the nurse said again.

"We're not done yet."

SARAH K. LENZ

I heard mumbled voices coming from the partition next to ours. It must have been Harper's family. I thought about what I might say when we passed them. What kind, encouraging words?

As we nursed, Stanley's energy returned, and I wondered if we had done the right thing. But how will I know if I made the right choice? That is the problem with parenting: there are too many variables to isolate. There's no provable cause and effect, only worry that, in the future, he will struggle. And when he does, I'll want to dig out the root cause. But now, in anticipation of imagined problems, I'm wracked with fear that I'm doing the wrong things, making poor choices. By the end of Olsen's story, the mother-narrator refuses the meeting with the guidance counselor. The ironing mother—as she runs the iron back and forth across the cloth—could have waffled: was I right or wrong? How should I have mothered her differently? But she doesn't. There isn't enough time "to sift, to weigh, to estimate, to total" because there is work to do, constant interruptions, and also the danger, she explains, that "I will become engulfed with all I did or did not do, with what should have been and what cannot be helped."

Kent hovered, standing above my shoulder. Stanley wiggled and gestured that he wanted to switch sides. He latched on to my other breast, and I thought about how hard, but necessary it is to summon up faith or my worry will drown out hope. When I have trouble praying, it's in those moments that God's plan feels distant, too unknowably mysterious. But isn't that situation of life itself? It's impossible to sift.

I snapped up my nursing bra. Kent gathered the diaper bag. I carried Stanley, and we walked toward the exit. I stopped at the next partition, but it was empty. Harper and his mother were gone. I wondered if he recovered or was transferred to a hospital. I wondered if he'd be okay. I wondered if Stanley would be okay. I wondered how I'd ever know when what "they" said was true. As I carried him out the door, Stanley patted my hair, then snuggled his face into the crook of my neck. Hope breaks through my doubt in moments when I'm flooded with sudden gratitude. At least I knew this: he'd made it through surgery with no complications. Even if the outcome remains unknown, I can hang onto this gratefulness, to see goodness in it. Perhaps that's as apt a definition of faith as any. But as I strapped Stanley into his car seat, it also occurred to me, like the best acolytes, it's better if I don't think too hard about it. Maybe some things we aren't meant to know. Especially now that the procedure is over, it cannot be helped.

PANCAKES ARE JUST PANCAKES

It is early December 2020 in South Texas, nine months into the COVID-19 pandemic. In my backyard, Meyer lemons hang heavy on their tree. Their deep yellow skins seem to glow from within. They are an unexpected miracle this season. We shouldn't have lemons at all, not yet. Kent and I planted the tree one balmy November afternoon. Stanley, five months old and new to sitting up, watched us from a blanket in the middle of the lawn as we dug into the thick, sticky clay soil. We stopped digging every time Stanley toppled to his side and fussed in frustration. The guy at the nursery told us we wouldn't get a harvest for five years, not until Stanley entered kindergarten, but now, only three years later, the small tree's branches bow under the weight of dozens of fist-sized lemons. They are a hopeful omen.

A few feet from the lemon tree, an ugly trench runs across the length of the yard. Mounds of jagged, black dirt hunker next to the twenty-five-yard-long gash across my lawn. A few days ago, we'd called a plumber to fix a minor water spigot issue that turned out to be a serious gas line leak. Seeing the earth dug up like this reminds me of a grave.

The COVID-19 virus keeps spreading, breaking out in waves of sickness everywhere in the United States, everywhere in the world. Every day, thousands of Americans die from it.

WHAT WILL OUTLAST ME?

Hospitals are overwhelmed. Shortages of medical supplies are common now—especially the ventilators that can keep COVID patients alive. During the hot summer months, our local morgues filled, so morticians used refrigerated semitrucks from FEMA to hold dead bodies.

Back in March, when the first lockdowns happened, it had been difficult to get basic goods: toilet paper, eggs, meat. Now the supply chain has recovered, but I still haven't been inside a grocery store in months. My small family took sheltering-in-place seriously, avoiding all contact with anyone who might infect us with this new virus. We pulled Stanley out of daycare. We pivoted to online-only remote work. When Stanley asks us why we can't go to the park or to the store, we say, "There are sick people there."

The rhythm of our lives has changed. I only leave home once a week for books and food. I pick up library books reserved online: picture books for Stanley, novels for me. I'm not allowed in the library. I'm required to wear a mask when the librarian meets me outside and places my books on a folding table. We maintain a distance of six feet. At the grocery store, I don't even leave my car for curbside service. I text my parking stall number to the store, and a masked employee comes out with my order and places the bags of groceries in my trunk without saying a word. In the Before Time, I used to pop into H.E.B. daily for a forgotten ingredient. Now I'm keenly aware of everything in the fridge. If I forget something, I do without. Nothing goes to waste anymore. This morning, I'd noticed half a tub of ricotta cheese leftover from lasagna. In the Before Time, it would have been ignored in the back of the fridge until it sprouted circles of orangey mold. My world has shrunk, so now I notice more.

SARAH K. LENZ

Then it hits me: I have all the ingredients for lemon ricotta pancakes.

Maybe I got the idea for pancakes because last night Stanley and I read a new library book, *If You Give a Pig a Pancake*. "If you give a pig a pancake," the book starts, "she'll want some syrup to go with it." The story continues with a series of if-then consequences that set off a chain reaction. Syrup will probably get her all sticky, so then she'll want a bath. If she wants a bath, then she'll want bubbles, and so on. Written in simple future verb tense, the book shows how simple actions can lead to wildly unpredictable experiences.

If I want lemon ricotta pancakes, then I'll have to pick lemons. If I go to pick lemons, I'll need to avoid the trench. If I don't avoid the trench, I'll think about awful, deadly things: how the trench costs thousands of dollars, how the gas line enters our home at the master bedroom, and how it runs through the foundation under our bed before it connects with the kitchen stove. Then I'll think about how if we hadn't caught the leak, there could have been a gas explosion while my husband and I were sleeping, and we would be dead. Then if I think about almost dying, I'll also think about how my mother, after finding out about our gas leak said, "This is an answer to prayer, because I pray for your every day." If the world is dangerous, then she'll pray for my safety. It's what mothers do.

If I think about mothers and dying, I'll remember an essay I read years ago about pancakes. The author, Marjorie Williams, diagnosed with terminal liver cancer and given a year to live, asks *how do you live when you have so little time left?* "What you do," she writes, "if you have little kids, is lead as normal a life as possible, only with more pancakes." I recall this passage, then I

WHAT WILL OUTLAST ME?

realize that's what I'm trying to do with my pandemic life: Make more pancakes.

If I ignore the trench, I'll notice the morning is gorgeous, and I do. My backdoor faces east, so as I walk from the house to the lemon tree, the sunrise greets me as it sparkles across dew-dappled grass. From the patio eaves, sparrows' flutter their wings and chirp. The air smells loamy and fresh. I breath deep. As soon as I pluck the first lemon off the tree, I sniff the sharp, clean perfume of its peel. A sense of fullness and love flows over me as I hold a bright yellow lemon to my nose and inhale it like a bouquet.

I don't understand this feeling, except it feels like a moment of awareness that a mysterious power holds everything together—the beauty, the pain, the lemon tree, the sparrows, me. It's as if I've stumbled across a conduit to God. My priest friend, Cynthia, reminds me: "Everything in creation has some imprint of God in it. You're just seeing God in creation." If you pick two lemons, then you may see God.

Mystics talk about moments like these as lifting the veil. Normally, my monkey mind hides this transcendent awe. In *Practical Mysticism*, Evelyn Underhill asks, "What is it that smears the windows of the senses? Thought, convention, self-interest." She likens it to fogging up the windowpane between ourselves and reality. William Blake makes the same point but uses a doorway metaphor. "If the doors of perception were cleansed," he explains, "everything would appear to man as it is—Infinite. But the doors of perception are hung with the cobwebs of thought, prejudice, cowardice, sloth." I've felt these sublime moments before. They occur when I'm still, when something unexpected occurred, or when I feel humbled by grief.

Even children can understand these moments when divine beauty breaks through the veil. I used to teach summer reading programs to fourth graders. We read *The Cricket in Times Square*. Chester Cricket lands in a New York subway station after getting trapped in a picnic basket. He befriends a young boy, Mario, who works at his family's failing newsstand. To improve business, Chester starts holding concerts. His music is so beautiful people compare him to Orpheus. But then, Chester gets homesick. Before he returns to Connecticut, Chester decides to hold a farewell concert. This last performance is poignant. Chester's song charms a crowded, bustling subway station to silent stillness. Everyone stops and listens, awestruck. In class, I always read this passage aloud, and the moment's magic always came through. Then, I asked my students: "When have you seen or heard something so beautiful it made you stop for a moment?"

I'm ready with my own example when students can't think of anything. One night when I was in college, I tell them, I drove home to central Nebraska to see my parents on a cold, gray November day. Just as I turned onto the road leading to their house, the sun broke through the clouds into the most magnificent sunset I'd ever seen. Red glowed on the horizon, but above it, slashes of orange blended into strokes of pink. Above that, huge puffy clouds soaked in deep shades of indigo and purple. I looked across a field of snow-covered cornstalk stubble, and the sky's brilliant colors sparkled off the snow too. I'd driven for hours in flat grayness, then this shocking sunset.

WHAT WILL OUTLAST ME?

"I had to pull the car over," I admit. What I don't tell my students is that was the night before Grandpa Harvey's funeral. I suspect if I had not been raw with grief, then the sunset would not have meant so much. A sunset was just a sunset, until someone I loved died. Pancakes are just pancakes, until something bad happens.

*

Back in the kitchen, I zest the lemons with a Microplane. The yolk-yellow skin flakes into the bowl like snow. I squeeze them in my citrus reamer. The juice bursts into the bowl. I add eggs, ricotta, milk, melted butter, and vanilla. Then I sift in flour, baking powder, salt.

While I wait for the electric griddle to heat (the gas stovetop is out of order, of course), I recall another time when transcendence overtook me. I was swimming. Many swimmers note how the combination of patterned breathing and decrease in sensory stimuli (skin waterlogged, goggles fogged, ears plugged) results in a meditative state. Roger Deakin writes, "When you enter the water, something like a metamorphosis happens. Leaving behind the land, you go through the looking-glass surface and enter a new world." I'm not sure if transcendence is a place my spirit goes (like through Blake's door) or an opening of awareness (wiping fog off Underhill's window), or a visitation from a God. Maybe it's all the above.

The last summer I lived in Georgia after finishing my MFA program, I felt the loss of leaving my friends to take a new job. Every day that summer, I swam in Lake Sinclair, alone, early in the morning. The lake's water stood still as glass, felt as warm as bathwater. One morning, it looked like rain, but I stubbornly kept my plan to swim anyway. By the time I donned a yellow swim cap and suit and arrived on the dock, fat rain clouds had crowded the sky. The lake water reflected a gray so soft and dense it seemed almost fur-like. I paused, listening for thunder and watching for lightning but detected neither, so I eased myself down the dock's ladder and began an Australian crawl. Fifty yards into my swim, I felt cold raindrops hit my cheek. I shivered. I wasn't just *in it,* I was *of it.* I broke my stroke. I treaded water. Bobbed like a buoy. The raindrops pelted down. They dazzled me with their dance. Droplets splashed on my face. I caught their beat. I danced too.

Maybe I perceived this unifying pulse of the universe because of the risk I took. My heartbeat pounded, more from excitement than exercise. Plunging into water during a rainstorm left me thrillingly vulnerable to a lightning strike. As my ears strained for the low rumble of thunder, and my eyes scanned the sky for flashes of light, I sensed something else. Proprioception, sometimes called the sixth sense, refers to our ability to know our kinetic parameters. As my limbs churned in place through the water, and raindrops drummed my skull, I looked up at the massive clouds in the sky, and the lake's horizon miles away, and what I sensed was how infinite creation is, how I'm a part of it too, but a small one. As my yellow swim cap covered head bobbed in the water, I felt as insignificant but as crucial as a speck of pollen inside a flower.

When both the college pool and the public Natatorium where I swim closed because of the COVID quarantine, I found other ways to exercise. I started meditating to try to find the same stillness and clarity I received from swimming laps in a slow, unbroken rhythm. In meditation, I find fleeting moments of connecting with a loving energy, which I've come to realize

WHAT WILL OUTLAST ME?

is God. Doing this is useful, like charging a dead spiritual battery, or glimpsing how I click into place within the universe, but it's not the same as touching a live spiritual wire. Transcendent moments have an ineffable spark.

The light on the griddle blinks green, indicating it's hot. I ladle out circles of thick, lemony batter that sizzle when they hit the griddle. The buttery smell of pancakes cooking wafts through the kitchen. If I want more of these moments—connection with all creation, soaking in the sacred, or unexpected awe—then I have to practice being open to them. If I am still, then something simple, yet sublime will probably happen.

Bubbles form and lightly pop on the raw surface of the pancakes. With a quick flip of my wrist, I flip them, revealing their golden sides like small suns. I stack them on white plates.

"Breakfast's ready," I call to Stanley, who's watching *Peppa the Pig* on the living room T.V. He scampers in, still in pajamas.

"Pancakes!" he says. "I want syrup too." I take out the maple syrup, and we pour generous puddles over our stacks. He stabs a forkful of pancake and takes a bite. I do the same. The pancakes turned out perfect: lemony, creamy, and fluffy.

"I just love pancakes, Mom," he says and takes another huge bite. His blond hair juts from his head in an adorable mop of blond curls. Another small pandemic surprise: when we stopped getting haircuts, we discovered Stanley's hair—if allowed to grow long—turns wildly, naturally curly. His blue eyes beam in the morning sunlight. He falls silent, concentrating on his meal.

SARAH K. LENZ

We sit and eat in companionable silence. I think about how a simple pancake reminds me life is brief, beautiful, and generous—even in the midst of pain. Pancakes are just pancakes unless you know you're going to die.

CANCER IS CLICHÉ

Thirty minutes after I was diagnosed with thyroid cancer, I wandered the aisles of Jo Ann's fabric shop because I didn't know what else to do. I'd had a good cry in my car parked at the medical center. I called my husband to break the news. He was calm and offered to drop everything to be with me, but I told it was okay. I had my to-do list. I'd go to Jo Ann's, which was what I'd scheduled to do after my doctor's appointment.

I'd had annual needle biopsies of my enlarged thyroid, and when the results showed a "neoplasm of uncertain behavior," I was sent to Dr. Weiss to have the left lobe of my thyroid removed. I liked the phrase "uncertain behavior." It wasn't as good as "benign," but Dr. Weiss told me I shouldn't be alarmed. "Less than 15 percent of cases like yours are cancer," he'd told me. I went to the appointment expecting a routine follow up. Then Dr. Weiss *dropped the bomb*, "The pathology report indicates you have a carcinoma." I felt all the clichés: *time stood still*; *I was caught off guard, taken aback,* and *frozen with fear.*

At Jo Ann's I paced the fabric aisles *in a daze.* I started in the quilting cottons. A rainbow whirled by. Vermillion, burnt umber, ochre. Chartreuse gave way to cerulean, then shifted to mauves and magentas. I moved from the quilting aisle to the apparel fabrics, touching each bolt. Crisp denims. Nubby chambrays. Cotton flannels like downy baby animals. Slippery chiffons and shimmering silk bolts cobbled in sequins. I rubbed my thumb and index finger over each one as if worrying prayer beads.

"When you're ill you instinctively fear a diminishment and disfigurement of yourself," writes Anatole Broyard. As I shuffled down the fabric aisles, I wondered, what would I become now that my thyroid is riddled *with cancer*? At thirty-seven, I was in a busy, vibrant stage of life, building a career I loved, raising a toddler, volunteering in my community, practicing hobbies like swimming and yoga. How could I be ill with cancer?

I had scheduled the diagnostic surgery at my most convenient time of year—after our family vacation but before I returned to teaching in the fall. Now at the end of summer, I wanted fabric to sew a new dress to wear back to school.

I circled a display of crepes. They had a pleasing texture. Finely pebbled. Grounding. The beautiful prints drew me in. One a deep mustard with violets, another navy with tiny magenta and gray scallops. *My mind raced, paralyzed by indecision.* Why in the hell are you buying fabric for a sewing project now that you have cancer? You think a new dress matters at a time like this? But why not? What else are you going to do? Be sick and bored? You deserve to treat yourself. Buy the fabric. Why make more work when you need to focus on your health? The voices in my head bickered. I took another lap around the store. Then I returned to the navy crepe and bought three yards of it.

Before my treatment began, I spent whole days obsessively researching differentiated thyroid cancers. I went straight for peer-reviewed medical journal articles with official-sounding

WHAT WILL OUTLAST ME?

titles: "Quality of Life in Thyroid Cancer Patients," "Differentiated Thyroid Cancer Survivors and Exercise," and "Clinical Epidemiology of Thyroid Cancer." My research unearthed paranoia. I felt wary of my body (why did a tumor grow in it?), of my pathologist (had he read the slides correctly?), of Dr. Weiss (why had he reassured me the tumor was likely benign?), and of modern medicine protocols (how would I know if we're taking the right course of treatment?) One Quality of Life Report even had the gall to say, "thyroid cancer is the real 'good' cancer," which I assumed was because its survival rates were high. Even if the immediate threat wasn't death, I was up against a list of chronic symptoms: uncontrollable weight gain, fatigue, menstrual complications, infertility, and brain fog.

The thyroid—and the hormones it produces—affects almost all body tissue. It regulates the rate and strength of heartbeats and the speed of metabolism, including appetite and gut motility. It's the body's thermostat. When I lost my thyroid to cancer, would I become like one of Edward Hoagland's turtles, "a kind of bird with the governor turned low"? Without a thyroid, I feared I'd morph into a different creature altogether, one slow, ugly, and unable to fly.

After reading too much bad news, I decided to cut out the fabric pattern pieces of the dress. The crepe was more slippery and delicate than it looked, and what I thought would be an easy task became frustrating. The fabric slid across the table and slipped away from the tissue paper pattern pieces. My shears struggled to slice a clean cut.

That evening after dinner, Kent and I watched the Red Sox game, but I only paid attention when an exciting replay flashed on the screen. I focused on my phone, Googling advice for thyroidectomy patients. My favorite site was a Facebook group called Active & Fit with No Thyroid. Members posted questions about medication doses, fitness goal triumphs, and even selfies in which they flaunted thyroidectomy scars as a survivor's badge. The group boasted 5,300 members, a fact I found comforting. *There's strength in numbers.* Less consoling were strings of posts lamenting gaining twenty-five, fifty, or seventy-five pounds. They lodged complaints about debilitating fatigue. Members griped about how their doctors didn't give a damn, refusing to change medication doses because blood work was good even though symptoms continued to diminish quality of life.

"There's a good chance I will experience significant weight gain—an average of thirty pounds," I read aloud.

"Well, hon," Kent said, "I always follow the 10 percent rule regarding anything you say."

"What do you mean?"

"You tend to dial everything up a notch, by about 10 percent. It's not lying. You have a mild, but chronic case of overreacting."

My spouse, who knows me better than anyone, has at least hit on my existential diagnosis. While he seemed to ignore the severity of my physical diagnosis, at least he got one thing right: I suffered from chronic hyperbole. His role in our eighteen-year partnership has been to talk me down from my exaggerations—especially when I go straight to the worst-case scenarios.

"I don't think you have anything to worry about. You work out too much. How many times a week do you swim laps?"

WHAT WILL OUTLAST ME?

"But that won't matter if my whole metabolism is short-circuited, or if I'm so exhausted, I can't swim anymore."

"You sound like your mother," Kent said. "I know you're going to be fine." He turned back to the ballgame. I wasn't mad that he compared me to my mother; I knew he was right. Mom Chicken-Littled things, and maybe I was doing it now too.

A week after my diagnosis only my husband and my mother knew. I wanted to hide the news. It was embarrassing to have cancer. I didn't want people to pity me, or worse, revere me as some sort of cancer saint. Cancer didn't feel like a spiritual cross to carry but something shameful that was all my fault. I hadn't eaten healthy enough nor 100 percent organic, nor exercised as well or frequently as I should have. I hadn't bought the expensive chemical free makeups and lotions, nor avoided enough carcinogens. I wrote about my cancer experience in my journal, but even that felt self-indulgent. I'd long scorned the cancer narrative because it is rife with worn out clichés. At a writing conference a couple of years ago, I heard the editor of a prestigious literary journal say, "Whatever you do, don't send us your cancer story. We will not publish it."

Finally, I drafted a social media post to announce my cancer news, but I sat on it for days before I finally posted it to Facebook and Instagram. Moments after I posted, my friend, Paul, who's a pathologist, messaged me: "You know, your kind of cancer is one of the most overdiagnosed. Head and neck cancers are my specialty. Do you want me to look at your slides?"

He explained to me that many pathologists over-call thyroid cancer cases. Perhaps that's what mine had done. I took him up on his offer. I just had to mail him the slides of thyroid tissue my first pathologist had seen.

After a string of frustrating phone calls, I was finally directed to go in person to the hospital's laboratory department. It'd been hard to find, located in the building's basement at the end of a labyrinthine set of hallways.

"This just isn't commonly done," the woman at the lab's counter sighed, frustrated at me for needing special forms she couldn't find. Finally, I signed all the paperwork she'd managed to dig up, and she handed me a small plastic case wrapped in bubble wrap, which contained twelve glass slides. It amazed me that my four-centimeter tumor had been reduced to a few transparent slices of tissue, and from these fragments, the doctors could determine if these cells were normal or cancerous.

On the way to the post office, the glass slides tinkled from where they sat on the passenger seat, reminding me everything is fragile. At the post office, when I handed the package to the postal clerk, I was afraid he would lose or damage the slides. James Brown's "I Feel Good" played from his phone on the counter and as the chorus belted from the tinny speakers, I thought with wry irony how physically I *did* feel good. I didn't feel ill at all.

"Anything liquid, perishable, or fragile?" he asked.

"Just fragile."

The clerk pounded a "Fragile" sticker on top of the priority envelope.

Paul called three days later. "I just looked at your slides," he said. "I agree with the first pathologist. It's cancer."

WHAT WILL OUTLAST ME?

I felt calmer than I'd expected. Maybe I *was* Sontag's stereotypical cancer patient: repressed, inhibited, numb. At least I had a second, certain opinion.

"If you want, I can make you a PowerPoint of the slides, so you can see for yourself." Paul knew I loved charts, diagrams, and statistics, and that I was comforted by facts and figures. A few hours later, he emailed me a PowerPoint presentation diagramming my cancer cells.

The thyroid tissue was tinted purple and pink, so the cells and follicles look like tie-dye or batik. The nuclei of cells bloomed between the slivers of glass like poppies. Paul had created maps with the slides. On the first, what appears to be a pink river, flowing in a diagonal current, is the tumor capsule. One side contains normal thyroid cells, and on the other—*the insurgent camp*. The tumor side of the river is distinct, filthy with dense purple dots. Those are the cancer cells. In another slide, Paul labeled where the tumor threatened to break free from its capsule and spread, creating a mushroom shape, *like an atom bomb detonating into the healthy tissue*.

The most overused metaphors for cancer come from war. Every good writer knows that overworked metaphors kill originality. Repeating an oft heard aphorism as one's own idea is a cop out. It's not earned wisdom. Even if some of the clichés ring true, they can't possibly define the whole story. Sontag's key argument in *Illness as Metaphor* is that our current metaphors for illness are themselves a plague. "The healthiest way of being ill is one most purified of, most resistant to, metaphoric thinking," she writes.

For some, though, metaphor is the only way of making sense of something so bewildering, so threatening to one's identity. Broyard argues, "Metaphors may be as necessary to illness as they are to literature, as comforting to the patient as his own bathrobe and slippers. At the very least, they are a relief from medical terminology...Perhaps only metaphor[s] can express the bafflement, the panic combined with beatitude, of the threatened person." Was this why I thought of Chicken Little's sky falling? Why I feared becoming turtle-like, even as I envied how they could retreat safely into a shell?

Since my mom was first diagnosed with breast cancer ten years ago, I've hated the way people described cancer with war language. "Your mom's a fighter. She'll win the battle against cancer," friends said. From my perspective, she wasn't fighting the cancer, but rather, skirmishing with the side effects of chemo and radiation. After her double mastectomy, she was so weak she couldn't bathe herself. My sister emptied her surgical drain tubes and gave her a bath. She saw firsthand cancer's disfigurement. Scars crossed mom's chest in angry jags of red, inflamed flesh. And even now, years later, I notice how her chest is cupped, concave like a shallow salad bowl, as if her heart-center has been carved out.

Cancer-as-war metaphors are so ingrained that even though I hated them, I could not separate their cliché imagery with cancer's literal meaning. After all, cancer truly is *a mutiny from within*. It starts with one rogue cell, which through a mutation in DNA, begins dividing at an abnormally fast rate, attaining unbridled growth. In normal cells, there are genetic circuits that regulate cell division and cell death, essentially preventing *a hostile takeover*. When that didn't happen and a carcinoma appeared, treatment was *to stop the cancer cell's campaign to spread and destroy*.

WHAT WILL OUTLAST ME?

Now that I knew I had an accurate diagnosis, I scheduled the first attack against my cancer: *extirpation*, to cut out by surgery, or a word used to imply extinction. The word in my mouth even sounded like a military strategy.

The second surgery was uneventful. The temporary medication Dr. Weiss prescribed—a strong preparation of synthetic T3 hormone—revved my metabolism and heartrate so much that I lost fifteen pounds. Next, Dr. Weiss referred me to a radiology oncologist, Dr. Voorhees, and explained he'd guide the next step in our *fight against cancer*, radioactive iodine ablation. Because thyroid cells absorb iodine to synthesize into hormones, oncologists found they *target-kill* (very *sniper-like*) thyroid cells that could be cancerous by giving patients an oral dose of radioactive iodine. Any stray thyroid cells that had survived extirpation would consume the poisoned iodine and *be annihilated by the radiation.*

I spent the weeks before my consultation with Dr. Voorhees researching and preparing. I would have to go on a low iodine diet, starving out those stray thyroid cells so they'd be famished for iodine and gobble up more radioactive iodine during treatment. After treatment, I'd be giving off enough radiation to be a danger to others, including Stanley, my fourteen-month-old son. I had a plan for my quarantine.

Behind our house, there is a mother-in-law apartment. Though we'd considered turning it into an Airbnb, we only use it as a guesthouse a couple of times a year when family visits. Mostly it's a storehouse for Kent's extensive comic book collection. I imagined how I'd spend four days in isolation reading Kent's comic books. I would over-identify with the superheroes who gain their powers from gamma ray exposure. I could set up my sewing machine and stitch together the fabric I bought on diagnosis day into a dress.

"You don't need any more treatment. You're done," said Dr. Voorhees at my long-awaited appointment. He talked fast, and when I asked questions, he went into professor-mode, which I instantly liked. He nodded with approval when I took out my notebook and started writing. He had prepared a thick stack of handouts as if he already knew how much I'd studied for this. He included the National Comprehensive Cancer Network's Treatment Guide, which I'd read during my research phase, but he interpreted for me. The treatment guide reads like a choose-your-own-adventure. Arrows forked down rows of treatment options as the route switched depending on variations within each type of thyroid malignancies. He led me through the diagram with my individual clinical factors: size of tumor, limited sites of capsular invasion, age at diagnosis, no evidence of metastases.

"Are you still with me?" he asked.

I nodded. He quickly flipped to the next page. This felt like a review, until he got to staging.

"You're at Stage I. This is good. We caught it early."

When we get to the final column of the final page of the flowchart, there is the final treatment recommendation: RAI is not typically indicated for patients having a low risk of recurrence/disease specific mortality.

Dr. Voorhees explained, "The risk of radioactive iodine ablation causing lymphoma or leukemia is greater than the

WHAT WILL OUTLAST ME?

probability that your thyroid cancer might reoccur. So, end of story," he said. "No RAI. And you won't be seeing me again."

"Wow. Okay." I smiled. *Relief washed over me*, and then (this is not a cliché) it destabilized me.

I knew I should be excited about my treatment being over, overjoyed that I would avoid the nasty side effects of RAI: permanent loss of taste, tear duct damage, saliva gland damage, increased risk of esophageal cancer. Now I was left unprepared for what was next. It didn't seem like after this small battle that *my fight against cancer* could be done. This unexpected change in course brought with it a crippling sense of uncertainty about my cancer story's ending.

I still wonder about that editor's prejudice against cancer narratives. I've come to believe that it isn't the stories themselves—some of them that flooded the editor's desk must have been well-written—but the fact that cancer leaves little room for a unique story. Beginning: diagnosis. Middle: treatment. End: death. My story was now stalled right after the second act. Treatment was over, but now what? Will cancer return? Will illness claim my life? I am faced—like we all are—with the uncertainty of mortality, for which the only closure is death. Arthur W. Frank writes, "Stories have to repair the damage that illness has done to the ill person's sense of where she is in life, and where she may be going. Stories are a way of redrawing maps and finding new destinations." But where, exactly, is my new destination?

My cancer felt like a detour—a cul-de-sac I got stalled in for a few short months. Yet one year out from my diagnosis, I'm still in *no-man's land*. I'm neither fully cancer free (I was turned away from donating blood at the Red Cross because the clinician said I might carry cancer cells), but I have no active tumors (they've been excised, and my bloodwork continues to indicate no active disease.)

Is my cancer story an initiation? Has my passage into cancerland made me more enlightened? "The romantic view is that illness exacerbates consciousness," explains Sontag. Cancer patients easily equate their heightened sense of mortality with enlightenment, which is why everyone's writing their cancer stories and sending them to that beleaguered editor. I had feared mortality before the diagnosis—and that fear got worse for a while—but now it's less crippling, and maybe as my fear of death fades, so does any spiritual illumination. Still, I will never return to my pre-cancer invincibility.

Living without a thyroid is a constant reminder that my health is precarious. My menstrual cycles have gone haywire, and the heavy bleeding causes anemia. My digestive tract has slowed, causing irritable bowel syndrome. A few months ago, the thyroid medication I rely on was recalled, but before I was notified of the improperly dosed medication, I developed terrifying heart palpitations, which could have caused a stroke.

It still takes frequent blood tests to regulate my thyroid levels, which are in a slow but constant flux. I'm in my optimum dose range more often than not, and when I am, I feel like my old self. Life continues. Even the eight-centimeter thyroidectomy scar at the base of my neck has faded to near invisibility.

Sontag believed that "the calamity of disease can clear the way for insight into lifelong self-deceptions and failures of character," and if that's true, I deceived myself by making meticulous, regimented plans. I had thought that if I'm

WHAT WILL OUTLAST ME?

worrying about and researching all the bad statistics that it would make a difference, as if that could somehow help me outwit death. I try not to not catastrophize so much, but I come from a long line of worrywarts.

My mother calls every time she goes in for routine monitoring.

"I'm getting my scan tomorrow. I just want you to know that I don't expect the results to be good. I'm sure I have another tumor."

"You don't know that," I tell her.

"I feel it," she says.

"Is there a lump?"

"No, it's just that it keeps me up at night, this feeling that I'm not well."

"I'm sure it's fine," I say, even though I know it's possible the sky is falling. "Let's wait to worry about it until the results come back."

I say this even though I know anxiety over cancer screening results can't just be switched off until after the scans confirm a carcinoma. My mother is right to worry. Cancer cells don't honor *ceasefire agreements.* Twice her cancer-cell *insurgents* have returned. They found another tumor a year after her double mastectomy, so she had another *extirpation,* chemo, and radiation. Then the same thing happened six years after that, more surgery, more radiation. One *pitched battle* after another.

This last time her scans were clean. I know the fear she lives with now that it's mine too. I understand the vigilance with which she watches and waits for the cancer to come back. It's a form of post-traumatic stress disorder. *Another wound inflicted by the cancer war.*

 We need new illness metaphors. About a year after my diagnosis, during a closet cleanout project, I found the crumpled fabric pieces for the navy blue dress I never made. As I pressed the pieces smooth again, I noticed a slub, a flaw in the fabric. Slubs are bumps projecting from the smooth fabric weave like a tumor. They're created when flying waste yarn gets into the yarn feeds when the cloth is spun. Slubs can be picked out, so I took a seam ripper and extracted the extra fiber, creating a burl mark, not unlike a scar left behind after surgery. Maybe this is my more apt cancer metaphor.

 I decided to stitch the dress together. When I tried it on, it wasn't like I expected. The pattern had an empire waist that jutted oddly from my hips. It didn't flatter my figure at all. I hadn't finished the neckline, armholes, or hem yet. Their raw edges could still unravel, but I had no desire to finish something if I wasn't going to like the outcome. I hung the dress in my closet. As I closed the door on it, I realized it felt like my cancer story, unfinished, but stopped, at least for the time being, from an unhappy ending.

FROM BIRTH TO BONE

The first dead body my son sees is a cat's. It was in his favorite parking lot. Since the stay-at-home orders were put in place when the pandemic started, we no longer feel safe at Lindale Park, so we come here—the rough asphalt parking lot of St. Luke's. Stanley enjoys riding his balance bike here, which he got for his third birthday a month ago in June. He's slow and cautious as he paddles his feet on either side of his first two-wheeler.

Out front, the marquee notes St. Luke's United Methodist Church offers online services at slumcorpuschristi.org. *They need a better social media manager*, I think at first, but then realize there might be an underhanded brilliance to it. Maybe a slum is where we notice God the most. It is, after all, where Jesus hung out.

This parking lot feels slummy. We often find empty forty ounce beer bottles swaddled in brown paper bags. Once by the back fence, we saw a used condom, curled and yellowing in the sun like a shed snakeskin.

"What this?" Stanley asked.

"A balloon," I said, which I supposed wasn't entirely false.

One afternoon, we discovered a homeless man napping behind the marquee. We weren't scared and didn't wake him.

The next day we saw a brand-new, bright orange sign tacked up on a tree trunk: *No Trespassing by order of Corpus Christi Police Department.* I wonder if the sign is meant for us, too.

*

A week later, we found the dead cat at the nicer end of the parking lot under a live oak tree. It lay between the curb and a clump of monkey grass on one side, and a parking block spray-painted with the word VISITOR on the other. In the heat of South Texas summer, we smelled it—the unmistakable stench of death—before we saw it. I looked at it with detached curiosity. A car must have run it over. Its eyes bulged. Its black fur ruffled in the breeze, flies crawled over entrails that had burst from its belly.

"What this?" Stanley asked, still astride his bike.

"It's a dead cat."

"What is dead?"

His question caught me off guard. I'd never thought to define it, not for Stanley anyway. I thought there'd be more time before tackling this question. I knew that putting death in relationship to its opposite by saying "not alive" didn't explain anything to a three-year-old.

"If something is dead, then it can't move," I said. "This cat isn't like Tessie at home, who pounces and plays and purrs because she's alive."

Stanley looked at me solemnly. I blurted out explanations because I didn't want him to fear death, and I didn't want to hide it from him.

WHAT WILL OUTLAST ME?

"Dead is what happens to a body. There's a part of us that lives forever called our soul. But I'm not sure what happens to it when we die."

"Oh," Stanley replied and rode off.

The next day when we returned to the parking lot, we found a turkey buzzard has arrived for a feast. Its talons ripped out the guts, then it slurped them like spaghetti. It seemed methodical and perturbed that we'd interrupted it.

"Go away, bird!" Stanley screamed. I thought about how my definition of dead deepens: Being dead meant you may become food, but I didn't try to explain this to Stanley.

The turkey vulture cocked its red head at us. I'd never seen one this close before, and it was huge. When it took off, its wingspan was easily six feet—a distance I'm a new expert at eyeballing—because we were never supposed to get closer than that to anyone who might infect us with the virus. I watched the vulture's slow wing beats. It soared to the church's art deco steeple in a dramatic sweep Alfred Hitchcock would have admired. At the base of the spire, it joined a dozen more vultures. I learned later that a group of perched vultures is called a wake because their heads hang down as if in mourning.

*

By January, six months after we first saw the dead cat, things have changed. Stanley is no longer hesitant on his bike. Now it's his monster truck, riding over concrete parking blocks, skidding to stops in fishtails that make gravel fly. Scattered among the pebbles, I notice bones. Sun-bleached and compelling. I am drawn to them, but I don't know why.

SARAH K. LENZ

I pick up a jawbone with a minuscule mountain range of jagged teeth. Fangs curled into parentheses. A flat scapula blade white as paper. A femur.

"What this?" Stanley asks.

"Bones. Remember the dead cat? Underneath all the fur and skin this is what's left."

"Let me pick one."

"Okay. Pick one. You have bones too, you know. Under your skin and muscles."

"And you?"

"Yes. I have bones too."

We sift through the loose dirt and gravel. He finds a leg bone. I take the two jaw bones and two vertebrae—each containing a perfect circle, where the spinal cord once flowed.

"Put in your pocket," he says, as he holds the bone out to me. I put them in the front pocket of my hoodie.

*

In February 2021, a month after we take the bones home, Texas is hit by an extreme cold front. The temperature drops below freezing and stays for days, breaking a twenty-year record. The power grid can't handle the strain, and we lose our electricity in rolling blackouts. Later the Texas Department of State Health Services reports that 210 people died of hypothermia during the freeze.

Our furnace cuts out, but we can light our gas stovetop with kitchen matches. It's our only source of heat. I make heavy comfort food that can be managed on the stovetop alone: chicken and dumpling soup, hot cocoa, and rice pudding sprinkled with cinnamon.

WHAT WILL OUTLAST ME?

We eat pancakes while our citrus trees in the backyard freeze to death, as the leaves of the star jasmine vine turn brittle and brown. A city water main freezes and breaks. There's a water boil alert. Our tap water slows to a trickle, so we open three-gallon jugs of stored water. We move our perishable food out to the frigid garage. Our four LED lanterns are fully charged, and they're bright enough to read by. Then, our cellphone service goes dead.

After months of digital hyperconnectivity through Zoom and the online learning management systems we use to work remotely, forced to make do with only analog feels calming. We sit together at the kitchen table. We roll Play-Doh into shapes with Stanley. We draw pictures using Magic Markers.

Kent and I have a bit more confidence improvising our lives because we've experienced other small disasters. The two hurricanes we've weathered, and the pandemic quarantines have taught us to make our home an island. We've learned to prepare for what we can control. For example, we're prepared with shelf-stable food and water for a week. We're still learning to let go of what we can't change.

Our utilities come back on for good after two and half days of rolling blackouts, and a few days after that, Stanley and I venture to Ropes Park, a small city park off Ocean Drive with bayfront access. To reach the water, we zigzag down a series of M.C. Escher-like steps made of railroad ties. There's a 100-yard strip of sand, and a wrack line often full of trash. We rarely encounter people here either, maybe because it's such a dirty beach strewn with plastic bottles, cigarillo tips, and odd shoes. I like this beach anyway. I like the way it's situated in the belly of the bay's curve, how huge boulders enclose it at either end. It's a hotspot for sea glass too. Stanley throws rocks into the surf and runs shrieking as the gulls dive and hover around our heads. The gulls must think we have food. Sometimes we bring our drive-thru lunches here because it's still not safe to eat in restaurants.

We're at the north end of the beach when we spot it. A sea turtle. For a while, I'd just thought it was another boulder, but no. It's a dead sea turtle tagged with a neon-orange X across it's back, indicating it's been counted in the Gulf's Sea Turtle Mortality Report. Its flippers and head are outstretched but look hollow like the flesh has been eaten from the inside out. I think of all the sea turtle rescue operation photos I'd seen on Facebook last week. Big pickup trucks with cargo beds filled with cold-stunned sea turtles to be warmed up, so they wouldn't freeze to death. Why wasn't this one rescued?

This time when Stanley sees the body, he says, "No, no, no. I don't like it. Let's go!" He grabs my hand, tugs me hard, away from the dead sea turtle. I don't want him to be scared, but he is. I feel helpless about the cruelty of the world, the type of cruelty that causes ordinary deaths every minute. I think of my Quaker friend, Janet, the first death doula I'd met. She'd sat with so many people while they were dying that death and suffering didn't scare her. Even when she admitted, "Death is a Great Mystery," she maintained a sense of awe rather than anxiety over the unknown.

As I slowly turn away from the sea turtle, I realize that seeing dead animals are my way of practicing compassion, which requires real presence. "Compassion is our capacity to relate in a tender and sympathetic way to what we perceive," writes Richard Rohr. He suggests that instead of "resisting our

WHAT WILL OUTLAST ME?

feelings of fear or grief," we should "embrace our pain with the kindness of a mother holding her child." I'm practicing, too, for when it's not an animal, but someone I love who's inanimate and breathless before me. Except there's no way to prepare for that sort of loss.

When the pandemic hit, my church started virtual prayer services. Ever since, I've tuned into a daily Facebook livestream of Compline—the bedtime liturgy from the Episcopalian Book of Common Prayer. The words from the prayer come to me unbidden: *Heal the sick, soothe the suffering, comfort the afflicted, and shield the joyful.* I've prayed that every night for a year. I'm still praying it. Ritual grounds me to the spiritual.

We leave the sea turtle and resume throwing rocks into the surf. It's so easy to turn away from something that is painful. I'm still not sure how to fight the urge to turn away, or why I feel like I shouldn't turn away. At my feet, I spy a piece of sea glass. My fingers graze the sand as I reach for it: a rounded, pale blue-green piece like a translucent robin's egg. I put it in my pocket.

When we return home from the beach, I put the sea glass on the bookshelf where I've made an altar of tokens we've collected on our walks: heart-shaped rocks, dove feathers, and small balls of Spanish moss. The cat bones sit in the center. I've arranged them symmetrically, like a face. Two round vertebrae form eye sockets, the femur looks like the bridge of a nose, and the jaw bones curve like cheeks. I put flat pieces of sea glass where I imagine teeth would go. Without exactly meaning to, I've made a *calavera*—a human skull-shaped symbol seen at Dias de Muertos celebrations. Come October, the stores in Corpus Christi will be full of colorful, festival skull representations on cookies, cakes, paper plates, and T-shirts. Here's another way to attend to death: with humor, a sly ironic smile. An attitude that shrugs and says, If you can't beat death, then you can at least be on friendly terms with it.

The significance of the cat bones keeps shifting on me. They comfort me with their solidness. Tommaso Fagioli writes, "Bones represent our truest and barest self…our home and anchor in the physical world." Bones exist as the last tangible thing after death. But the cat bones scare me too because they look so much like my bones. Those cat vertebrae I hold in the palm of my hand are the same shape as the bone knitting my spine together, aren't they?

I never took anatomy and physiology in college, and I was always a little envious of those that did with their coloring-book study aids, a neat row of colored pencils, and those diagrams labeling every part of the human body. All this precision and we still don't know where the soul resides. We still don't know what happens to the spirit when someone—person or animal—breathes its last.

One day in mid-March, a full year into the pandemic, Stanley scoots a chair to the bookcase so he can reach my altar. Before we pulled him out of preschool to shelter-in-place, his teachers used to designate time for play with loose parts: buttons, beads, and rocks, that kids can engage in imaginative play. To him, my sacred objects are just loose parts.

Stanley sweeps the sea glass over the side, then moves the cat bones, obliterating my *calavera*.

"This is the momma bone," he says, holding one of the jaw bones. "And this is the daddy bone." He points to the largest one, the femur.

WHAT WILL OUTLAST ME?

"What's this one?" I point to a vertebra.

"The kid one!"

As I watch him play, I think about how I'm moving on this life circle and so is Stanley. Like the cat, the homeless man, the turtle, and the turkey vulture.

Last night we saw turkey vultures again. Kent was washing dinner dishes when he spotted two dozen turkey vultures roosting in the bare red oak trees across the street.

"Look, Hon!" Kent called, and he dried his dish-soapy hands and grabbed his camera. Photography was his new pandemic hobby. I peered out the window at the wake of hunched birds silhouetted against the dusky sky and I thought: *what's died now?*

"Let me come too!" Stanley shouts, so we put on shoes and headed down the street. We were in the golden hour photographers covet, the time just past sunset when light is soft and diffused making any subject look beautiful. Neighbors have come out to watch. The shutter of Kent's camera shutter *tkk-tkked*, mechanically. Stanley held my hand.

"So many birds, Mama!" He pointed to a dozen more turkey vultures circling in the sky, floating on thermals. They swirled downward in a funnel until they found a place to perch for the night: an old telephone pole in the alley, a scraggly backyard palm tree, or the branches of the oak tree on the corner.

"Look at the hawks," a man with a white beard yelled from across the street. "There must be forty or fifty of them."

"Those aren't hawks," I yelled back. "They're turkey vultures."

"Are you sure?"

"Yes, see their bald, red heads?" I wanted to add that there must be a dead animal nearby, why else would they be here? I pulled out my phone, wanting to prove I'm right, even though I wouldn't dare get near enough to show him my phone screen because he might be infected with the virus.

"I've never seen anything like this," he shouted.

"Me either." We probably wouldn't have even noticed the vultures if not for the pandemic that narrowed the scope of our lives.

A quick Google search revealed that these turkey vultures were migrating. Because the birds glide on updrafts, they love flying along shorelines where the temperature shifts between land and sea create great thermals. In March and November, Corpus Christi is on the vulture migration superhighway. These birds would eventually stop somewhere in the Midwest, their summer breeding grounds. This time they aren't here because death lurks, they're on their way to make babies.

*

Balanced on the edge of the chair, Stanley uses the cat femur to shove a green piece of sea glass off the bookcase. It clatters to the hardwood floor. I scoop it up and put it back.

"Okay. You need to get down now," I say, but he's still engrossed by the bones.

"Not yet. *Muh-rrrr!*" He zooms a bone across the shelf. "*Muh-rrrrrr.* It's a car!"

WHAT WILL OUTLAST ME?

"Drop it. Or the tickle monster will get you!"

He squeals. I grab him, wrapping my arms around his waist, and scoop him up in a monkey-hug while I tickle his armpits. He giggles, big, burbling, hiccup-gulping giggles. He drops the femur back on the shelf. It makes a soft, hollow clatter as it hits the wood, returning to a memento, reminding me that the cycle from birth to bone is brief, but brilliant.

BEFORE IT'S NIGHT ONCE MORE

I found the lump because I wanted to get pregnant with you. Every morning for two years, I'd looked at my goiter in the mirror. At the base of my neck, it was a squashed racquet ball, a baby turtle shell, a goose egg. The ultrasounds said that it was only four centimeters in diameter, but when I tilted my head back and arched my neck, it looked much larger, lodged just above my clavicle. It protruded from my throat, both firm and squishy. It had been with me since I started thinking about you.

Your papa and I had waited to start a family until we finished graduate school, had good jobs, and had saved enough money to put a down payment on a house. I had done my homework. All the prenatal books advised: Make an appointment with an OB/GYN before you start trying to get pregnant. I went to the doctor and told her I wanted to get pregnant, and the first thing she said was, "Well, you're of advanced maternal age, so your risk of having a baby with Down Syndrome is much higher." She handed me a photocopied chart with the statistics. I was thirty-five. (My risk: 1 in 350, just where the line graph arched steeply upward.) The chart had been copied from copies so many times that the words blurred, and grainy dots of Xerox toner stained the paper.

As I sat on the exam table wearing a brittle paper gown while the doctor looked in my ears and throat, I thought about

WHAT WILL OUTLAST ME?

how she implied I was too old to have a baby. If I conceived you, and something went haywire with one of your chromosomes, it would be my fault because I had waited too long to be ready for you.

"Uh-oh, something's going on here with your thyroid," the doctor said as she palpated my neck and found the lump. She told me to make an appointment with my primary care physician.

"What's wrong?" I asked. She told me my thyroid was abnormally enlarged.

A few days later, sitting on the exam table at my primary care physician's office, I asked Dr. V. the only thing I could think about since the lump was pointed out: "Is it cancer?"

"It's possible, but not likely," he told me. (I checked the statistics. Of all cancer cases in the U.S., 3.8 percent of them are thyroid cancer.) My doctor ordered a battery of tests. Bloodwork, ultrasound, biopsy.

I went back a week later for a follow-up visit when the results were in: the biopsy was negative and the blood work showed that my thyroid was producing all the hormones it was supposed to, at all the appropriate levels.

"What if I want to get pregnant?" I asked. (I had also checked: in a potentially flawed and controversial study of 168 mothers with thyroid disease, "18 percent of the babies had serious birth defects, ranging from heart problems to cleft palate and extra fingers.")

"Then get pregnant," Dr. V said with a nonchalant shrug.

So I did. With you. As soon as your papa and I started trying. It was as if you'd been waiting so long that you took the first opportunity we gave you. It felt like a risky gamble against the Down Syndrome odds, against all manner of congenital diseases, but more things in life are a gamble than we realize.

I found a new OB/GYN, Dr. Shelton, who never told me that I was too old. She ordered blood tests every six weeks to make sure my thyroid was humming along so you would grow perfectly. And you did. My thyroid goiter grew too, an expanding smooth lump nestled above my collarbone. If the light caught it right, like in a photograph, it seemed to glow, a white bulb at the base of my neck.

Deciding to have you was the greatest act of faith I have committed. I was tested for anemia, gestational diabetes, Rh factor, HIV, hepatitis B, syphilis, and rubella. My doctor screened for urinary tract infections and high blood pressure. We'd run all the genetic tests and Down Syndrome came back negative. Gradually, as my pregnancy with you progressed uneventfully, as test after test confirmed my good health and your good health, I eased into an attitude of surrender. I gave my body gladly over to the process, amazed at my magnificent melon-belly.

We took a natural childbirth class. I was taught how to relax and trust my body. Be patient with the natural course of things. I learned I should shun the doctors when they tried to convince me I needed Pitocin to speed things up, an epidural to ease the pain, and a C-section if things were still taking too long or if there was some doubt my body wouldn't function as it was supposed to.

WHAT WILL OUTLAST ME?

The day before I went into labor, I sat in Dr. Shelton's office so pregnantly engorged it felt like I was sitting directly on your head. She told me that you might get stuck in my birth canal. An ultrasound that morning revealed that your shoulders were wide, and they might catch on my pelvis. That afternoon I researched shoulder dystocia, even though your papa wasn't worried. He said, "Our baby's just barrel chested like all Lenz men." He, his brother, and his father had all been born vaginally, broad shoulders and all.

I was worried. When a shoulder dystocia happens, the doctor must try to rip the baby out of the birth canal within five minutes of birth or there will be brain damage or even death. They will use any means necessary: cutting open the vaginal walls, cracking the baby's collarbone and wrenching the arm until it breaks free from the grinding shoulder bone on pelvic bone trap. Most babies who suffer shoulder dystocia have nerve damage and suffer permanent arm paralysis. Some have significant intellectual delays because oxygen gets cut off from their brain. There's no real way to know for sure if it will happen before it's too late, but it's also relatively rare. (Current statistics suggest "shoulder dystocia occurs in 0.2 to 3 percent of deliveries.") Before I could contemplate risks and odds, and whether we should schedule a C-section, I went into labor.

At the hospital, after twenty-hours of active labor, the doctor on-call stood at the foot of my bed.

"I suspect you're not progressing because the baby's shoulders are too large," the doctor said. She paused while I rode the wave of another contraction. A sharp pain tried to crack me open, to take me into another realm of existence. She continued, "I'm never afraid of C-sections, but shoulder dystocias scare me."

The doctor had brought along a nurse, and she chimed in. "My sister was a shoulder dystocia. It's affected every aspect of her life." Her face was grim with the sorrow of this testimony.

Between contractions, I discussed the situation with your papa. Together we argued out a compromise with the doctor. I agreed to let her strip my membranes to try to speed things up. She took a long, flat, plastic rod that looked like a knitting needle and broke my water. This intensified the pain of contractions. The fetal monitor showed you were in distress, so they made me wear an oxygen mask. I was terrified everything was going wrong.

In the space of those next few hours, as the pain got worse, there was a moment. Maybe even an epiphany. I'd read accounts of women saying giving birth is as close to death as you get without dying. "When a woman gives birth, death holds her hand for a little while," wrote Betty Smith in *A Tree Grows in Brooklyn*. In Elisa Albert's *After Birth*, she describes labor as a processed that "approached death. You go down into places it's hard to get at in life, you know? Extremity. And there's no safe word. No, like, 'stop this train, I want to get off.' My soul left my body. Ego firebomb. I thought I was exploding. Like literally: becoming a star."

Yeah, sure, whatever, I'd thought dismissing these descriptions as the hyperbole inherent in novels. They didn't have the firm logic I craved from statistics. But now I know it's true. Something in my psyche broke loose. Was this death drawing near? My ego being firebombed? An idea popped into my brain, what some people would call a message from the

WHAT WILL OUTLAST ME?

Divine. *If you die or if your baby dies, it is fate. You have no control over it. If your baby has shoulder dystocia, it's meant to be. And if so, that will be the way he lives and learns and exists, and anyway, that's the way life is—unpredictable.*

Your papa stayed by my side the whole time. I knelt on all fours on the floor by the bed, desperate for a position that would be more comfortable. A nurse came to check my cervix.

"It's okay to push now," she told me. It felt like your head through my pelvis was nothing but a squiggling ball of energy, trapped, and trying to get out in an angry rush. When I pushed, I timed my breath the way our childbirth instructor had said, breathing in deeply with the rise of the contraction. I was an animal, summoning energy from my throat. Just as you crowned, the doctor made me flip to my back, feet in stirrups. She wanted to be ready to pry your shoulders out of me. But then, you slipped out. Here you were. Bright pink, lungs full of air.

The next day we went home—blindsided by fatigue and the rush of love—but also sheepish. Why had we worried so much? And how had we been so stubborn, so brave, so utterly trusting that everything would work out okay? Maybe we'd been reckless. Maybe, we thought, it was just dumb luck. All that worry now seemed for nothing. It is a cruel trick of fate that we always seem to worry about the wrong things.

Those first few weeks of your life, I knew my goiter grew worse. It ached. It stretched the skin of my neck taut. I went back to the doctor. Dr. V palpated the mass on my neck, then he pulled a little plastic ruler out to measure it.

"Wow. That's a big goiter," he said, then sent me to an endocrinologist, Dr. Amaral.

"Your immune system is attacking your thyroid cells, and in defense, your thyroid is producing more and more cells to compensate, which is why it's enlarged," Dr. Amaral explained when I asked about the newest round of test results. She had kind eyes and wore expensive shoes. "This lobe of your thyroid has to go," she declared.

When I asked why we couldn't consider a less invasive treatment, she said that needle biopsies weren't very accurate, and that the damaged lobe would keep growing, and at the rate the cells were multiplying, one of them was likely to become cancerous. My odds looked good. (Only about 10-15 percent of thyroid nodules like mine prove malignant.)

"How can I have surgery if I'm breastfeeding?"

"You can wait," she said, "until your son is a little older."

I scheduled the surgery for a month after your first birthday. I had never been under general anesthesia before. I was worried I wouldn't wake up. These things happen, I knew. (Anesthesia-related mortality rates are 0.4 out of 100,000). In the weeks leading up to the surgery, I thought about my legacy to you. What would you want to know if I died before you were old enough to remember?

I decided you needed a baby book. I culled through my journal entries from the past year, copying and pasting any passage about you into a self-publishing app, and adding pictures until I had 150 pages. I wrote about the mundane details of our first year together. The saga of breastfeeding and sleep patterns. Your first foods, your first steps, and all your typical baby milestones. I had it printed by a vanity publishing company, but I didn't feel vain because I'd tried to be honest about how I felt as a new mom and not sentimental. I imagined,

WHAT WILL OUTLAST ME?

someday, in the far future you will be fascinated (or perhaps mortified) by this book. Perhaps you'll read it right before you have kids of your own. Maybe you'll see it as too much information, too uncensored. Did I really need to record how your little penis got a nasty rash from a yeast infection when you were 6 weeks old? If you ever read those pages, you'll find my longing for posterity, for a legacy to survive beyond me. What will outlast me, if not my words, and if not you?

The morning of my surgery, you, Papa, and I arrived at the same hospital where you were born. It was so early your daycare wasn't open yet. The pre-op room was dimly lit. The nurse handed me a paper hospital gown and a pair of purple socks with puff-paint grippers on the bottom. The grippers were shaped like two bears hugging: a momma bear and cub. Papa was barely awake, sipping coffee from his thermos. While we waited, I nursed you. I knew it would be our last chance for a while. The anesthesiologist said it would be at least twenty-four hours before the drugs would clear my system, and then it'd be safe for you to suckle again.

After you were done nursing, we still waited. You, like thirteen-month-olds are wont to do, became squirrelly. You wanted to run. You wanted to grab: my IV line, the strings of my gown, the trashcan. There was a crucifix and a clock on the wall, and as the hands of the clock clicked closer to the time they would wheel me off to the OR, you started fussing more.

"Daycare's open now. Should I take him now and come back?" your Papa asked.

"Yes," I said, even though I knew it meant I'd be alone. I kissed you and told you I loved you.

When they wheeled me into the OR, I saw a cloth-draped table laid with hundreds of shiny surgical implements, like a gigantic silverware stash, and I thought about how much you would love to grab each one, like the way you grab silverware from the dishwasher basket. I saw the purple foam block where I would lay my head, like my yoga blocks at home you play with. Underneath my thoughts of you, a flat fear spread as I tried not to think about what would happen to me on the table, the way the front of my neck would be sliced into. I laid down on the operating table, and they spread my arms out like a crucifix. The anesthesiologist appeared above my head with a gas mask. Before I lost consciousness, she said, "Kiss that beautiful baby for me."

I came to in the recovery room vomiting bright yellow bile. The surgery was successful. It hurt when I swallowed, like having a bad case of strep throat, but I refused pain meds so I could nurse you sooner.

That evening, Papa brought you to see me. You crawled around on my hospital bed and played with my IV line—the colorful plastic clips dangling from its cord. We shared a pint of mint ice cream your papa brought.

The next morning, I was discharged from the hospital. When I came home, and you saw me, you burst into tears of relief. You wanted to nurse. I wasn't supposed to lift you, but I did, carefully, drawing you up onto the couch where I sat. You latched on quickly, and we were content. I breathed in the top of your head, which smelled like baby powder. Your curious hand reached up to my neck and tried to pat the surgical tape covering my incision, but I intercepted it and held your tiny fist with its perfect knuckle dimples.

WHAT WILL OUTLAST ME?

A week later, at my surgical follow-up appointment, Dr. Weiss, handed me the pathology report of my thyroid lobe.

"They found a carcinoma," he said. "Not what we were expecting."

Expecting. I think of how we used that word during pregnancy. "I'm expecting," I had said. It was another way to say I imagine a future, our future together.

"We'll need to remove the other thyroid lobe, to be sure we've excised all the cancer," he explained, while I felt frozen. But then, Dr. Weiss spoke in the comforting language of statistics.

"Once you've had a total thyroidectomy," he said, "the probability that your cancer ever reoccurs is less than 1 percent."

My prognosis is good. (The five-year survival rate is almost 100 percent for localized follicular cancers like mine). Thyroid cancer is very treatable, and they found mine while it was still encapsulated in thyroid tissue, which was surgically removed. But just like the doctors couldn't know for certain if you'd be a shoulder dystocia, they don't know when or if my cancer might come back. We are in the wait and see phase of treatment. Just like in pregnancy, there will be vigilance and monitoring. Scans and bloodwork every six months, checking in, looking for a lethal malignancy. There's a nervous expectancy, but in the meantime, there's so much life to live with you.

What if I hadn't wanted you? If I hadn't hoped to get pregnant with you, would I have found the lump before it was too late? In creating you, I created another storyline in my life. Perhaps I'll have extra chapters in my life because of you.

SARAH K. LENZ

It's a month after my surgery, and you've just said your first words: ball and kitty. You've cut your twelfth tooth, and you're learning to use a spoon. You can climb on top of the coffee table now, and you watch for me to catch you when you jump off, and then you giggle. I keep recording these things in my journal. I record other things, too. One day I copied down a line from Maggie Nelson's *Bluets*: "That the future is unknowable is, for some, God's means of suturing us in, or to, the present moment." That's the best way I know to avoid fearing my mortality: stay mindful, knitted to this present moment. I keep writing down as many of these moments as I can.

The thing they never told me in childbirth class is that by bringing a life into the world, I have also, inevitably, created a death. We die simply because we were born. There's a famous Samuel Beckett line from *Waiting for Godot*: "One day we were born, one day we shall die, the same day, the same second... Birth astride of a grave, the light gleams an instant, then it's night once more." Many critics say the play is absurdist, supposedly championing the belief that we are incapable of finding life's meaning. But I don't see it that way. It's a reminder that life is short, but so full of gleaming moments: the way your face lit up the first time you tasted a strawberry, the chatter you make discovering words, the way you giggle when I tickle the right spot under your chin. Is it purpose enough to soak up these experiences? Maybe we are here to experience love, to drink in what it means to be alive, this joy—that for the

WHAT WILL OUTLAST ME?

time being—we have a body that can see and taste and touch and smell and hear. How glorious! I want to show you these gleaming moments for the rest of my life because I knew long before you could comprehend, they can be gone in an instant. Let's you and I live as much as we can before it's night once more.

NOTES

DRIVING THE SECTION LINE

Page 17: "...during the Earl Butz era of American agriculture, the beginning of rapid consolidations and the "get big or get out" mentality: "Farm Bust of the 1980s," *Living History Farm*, accessed 1 November, 2021, https://livinghistoryfarm.org/farminginthe70s/money_05.html

LIGHTNING FLOWERS

Page 47: "Capture special moments of love for parents experiencing the loss of an infant. Your precious gift provides healing for a family while honoring the baby's legacy": "Give the Gift of Heirloom Remembrance Portraits," *Now I Lay Me Down to Sleep*, accessed October 26, 2021, https://www.nowilaymedowntosleep.org/.

Page 49: **Mother Holds Daughter with Rigor Mortis:** Stanley Burns, *Sleeping Beauties: Memorial Photography in America*, (Twelvetrees Press, 1990).

Page 49: **Lichtenberg figures, named after the German physicist who in 1777 studied the patterns high voltage static electricity made:** "Lichtenberg Figure, "*Wikipedia*, last modified on 13 September 2021, at 19:31, https://en.wikipedia.org/wiki/Lichtenberg_figure.

Page 50: "However lightning-like it may be, the *punctum* has...a power of expansion": Roland Barthes, *Camera Lucida: Reflections on Photography*, (Hill & Wang, 2010), 53. First Published 1979.

Page 51: "We photograph things in order to drive them out of our minds": Kafka qtd in Barthes, *Camera Lucida*, 53.

Page 53: "We are drawn to the dead and yet abhor them….We love and hate them all at once": Thomas Lynch, *The Undertaking: Life Studies from the Dismal Trade*. (W.W. Norton, 2009).

Page 55: "In the US between 1910 and 1919, out of every million people 4.5 were killed by lightning": Ronald L. Holle, "Annual Rates of Lightning Fatalities by Country." 20th International Lightning Detection Conference. 2008, accessed September 30, 2021, https://www.vaisala.com/sites/default/files/documents/Annual_rates_of_lightning_fatalities_by_country.pdf.

Page 56: "One out of eight American women, or 12 percent, will be diagnosed": "Genetics," *Breast Cancer.Org*, accessed October 26, 2021, https://www.breastcancer.org/risk/factors/genetics.

Page 56: "Let us have nothing on our minds as often as death": Montaigne qtd in Sarah Bakewell, *How to Live: Or a Life of Montaigne in One Question and Twenty Attempts at an Answer*. (Other Press, 2011). First Published 2010.

Page 56: Its literal translation from the Latin far less congenial: Remember that you will die. "Memento Mori." *Wikipedia*, last updated October 15, 2021, at 02:52, https://en.wikipedia.org/wiki/Memento_mori.

SHOOTING ON IZARD STREET

Page 65: "My husband is shooting. My four-year-old is still in the house": Karyn Spenser and Christopher Burbach,

"Slain Man's Actions Puzzle Family," *Omaha World-Herald*, July 17, 2001.

Page 68: **But 9/11 was different than the shooting. It made us collectively, as Americans, all vulnerable:** My understanding of collective vulnerability and the way fear drives us to dismiss certain lives as not worthy of mourning came from Judith Butler, *Precarious Life: The Powers of Mourning and Violence*, (Verso, 2006).

Page 70: **Zimmerman's jury believed he had been threatened to the point of needing to defend himself:** Lizette Alvarez and Cara Buckley. "Zimmerman Is Acquitted in Trayvon Martin Killing." *New York Times*. July 13, 2013. https://www.nytimes.com/2013/07/14/us/george-zimmerman-verdict-trayvon-martin.html.

KILLING CHICKENS

Page 71: **a town of 30,000:** "Bowling Green, Ohio," *Wikipedia*, last updated on July 31, 2021, at 03:16, https://en.wikipedia.org/wiki/Bowling_Green,_Ohio.

MAKING HEADCHEESE

Page 87: **"...savory wink...sense of gastronomical freedom"**: M.F.K. Fischer, "How to Carve the Wolf," *The Art of Eating*, (Wiley, 2004), First Published 1937.

Page 94: **"Why is it worse?..."**: M.F.K. Fischer, "How to Carve the Wolf."

Page 95: **"When you eat a stuffed baked bull's heart, or a grilled lamb's brain...you need not choke them down with** nauseated resolve...but with plain delight.": M.F.K. Fischer, "How to Carve the Wolf"

A BOOK FROM MY GRANDMA, A MESSAGE FROM THE GRAVE

Page 102: "...liked the pawnshop...treasure prodigiously thrown": Betty Smith, *A Tree Grows in Brooklyn*, (Harper & Brothers, 1943).

Page 104: "A head pain caught her between the eyes at the taking in of such a wonderful sight. It was something to be remembered all her life": Betty Smith, *A Tree Grows in Brooklyn*.

Page 105: "Sometimes it seems to me that as a way of thinking grief has much in common with speculative fiction...": Sandra Gilbert, "E-mail to the Dead," *Death's Door: Modern Dying and the Ways We Grieve,* (W.W. Norton, 2006).

Page: 105: "fascinated and revolted.... He was a baby once...": Betty Smith, *A Tree Grows in Brooklyn*.

Page 107: "As we survivors journey into our own futures...": Sandra Gilbert, "E-mail to the Dead," 66.

Page 107: "To die is different from what any one supposed, and luckier...": Walt Whitman from *Leaves of Grass* qtd in Sandra Gilbert, "E-mail to the Dead," 72.

Page 108: "The last time of anything has the poignancy of death itself...": Betty Smith, *A Tree Grows in Brooklyn*.

Page 108: "Death is the end of all story...it is what is 'impossible to tell'": Walter Benjamin, from *Illuminations* qtd in Sandra Gilbert. "E-mail to the Dead," 97.

HOLY DIMINISHMENT

Page: 113: "After we are in the new house, memories of other places we have lived in come back to us…": Gaston Bachelard, *The Poetics of Space: The Classic Look at How We Experience Intimate Places.* (Beacon Press, 1994), 5-6, First published 1958.

Page 116: "Place possesses you in its absence…they become deities.": Rebecca Solnit. *A Field Guide to Getting Lost,* (Penguin, 2005).

Page 119: "If you are to hallow diminishment, it is necessary to fill your life…": John Yungblut, *On Hallowing One's Diminishments.* (Pendle Hill Pamphlet 292, 2013), First published 1990.

Page 126: **A little boy finds a butterfly struggling and thrashing in effort to get out of its cocoon…:** Nikos Kazantzakis, *Zorba the Greek.* (Simon & Schuster 2014), 142. First published 1946.

I first heard this story during a twelve-step meeting, but it wasn't until many years later that I stumbled across its source and realized the boy's meddling was even more gentle that I'd remembered, but just as devastating. Here's the original parable:

"I recalled one dawn when I had chanced upon a butterfly's cocoon in a pine tree at the very moment when the husk was breaking and the inner soul was preparing to emerge. I kept waiting and waiting; it was slow and I was in a hurry. Leaning over it, I began to warm it with my breath. I kept warming it impatiently until the miracle commenced to unfold before my eyes at an unnatural speed. The husk opened completely; the butterfly came out. But never shall I forget my horror: its wings remained curled inward, not unfolded. The whole of its minuscule body shook as it struggled to spread the wings outward. But it could not. As for me, I struggled to aid it with my breath. In vain. What it needed was to ripen and unfold patiently in sunlight. Now it was too late. My breath had forced the butterfly to emerge ahead of time, crumpled and premature. It came out undeveloped, shook desperately, and soon died in my palm.

This butterfly's fluffy corpse is, I believe, the greatest weight I carry on my conscience. What I understood deeply on that day was this: to hasten eternal rules is a mortal sin. One's duty is confidently to follow nature's everlasting rhythm."

Page 127: "We enjoy contemplating the most precise images of things whose actual sight is painful to us, such as the forms of the vilest animals and of corpses": Aristotle, *Poetics* 1448b qtd in Nigel Gaut Berys and Dominic Lopes, eds. *The Routledge Companion to Aesthetics.* (Routledge, 2005), 208.

Page 129: "The extraordinary excites but alarms us...we regain equilibrium": Rosemarie Garland-Thompson, *Staring: How We Look*, (Oxford University Press, 2009).

Page 131: "The spectre of our eventual becoming object...is a shadow that accompanies us throughout our lives": Maggie Nelson, *The Art of Cruelty: A Reckoning,* (W.W. Norton, 2012).

Page 132: "You find them bending over photographic views .... chained by the strange spell that dwells in dead men's eyes": "Brady's Photographs; Pictures of the Dead at Antietam," *New York Times*, October 20, 1862, https://www.nytimes.com/1862/10/20/archives/bradys-photographs-pictures-of-the-dead-at-antietam.html.

Page 132: **Brooklyn School Children See Gambler Murdered in the Street (1941)**: "Weegee: Their First Murder." *International Center of Photograph,* accessed October 19, 2021, https://www.icp.org/browse/archive/objects/their-first-murder-1.

Page 133: In 2000, curator James Allen opened *Without Sanctuary,* an exhibition that gathers over a hundred photographs of lynchings taken between 1882 and 1965: James Allen and John Littlefield, *Without Sanctuary: Photographs and Postcards of Lynching in America,* accessed October 5, 2021, https://withoutsanctuary.org/

Page 134: "It wasn't the corpse that bewildered me as much as the canine-thin faces of the pack, lingering in the woods, circling after the kill": James Allen and John Littlefield. *Without Sanctuary.*

This quote is from the original movie I showed my composition students and is available on this website, and though, painful to view, I still see it as integral to understanding the history of racial atrocity in the United States.

Page 135: **Georgia College...is 80 percent white and only 8 percent Black:** "Georgia College & State University," Data USA, accessed November 1, 2021, https://datausa.io/profile/university/georgia-college-state-university.

Page 135: **Viewing violent scenes doesn't prevent future violence. It makes the viewers feel invulnerable:** Susan Sontag, *Regarding the Pain of Others,* (Farrar, Straus and Giroux, 2003).

Page 137: "Surely what we should wish for is a world where the vulnerability of the beholder is equal to or greater than the vulnerability of the person beheld...": Elaine Scarry,

On Beauty and Being Just, (Princeton UP, 2001), First published 1999.

Page 138: "We experience the Sublime when we confront the awful contingency of nature....**"Anything which alters consciousness in the direction of unselfishness, objectivity, and realism is to be connected with virtue.**": Iris Murdoch, *The Sovereignty of Good,* (Routledge Classics, 2001), First published 1970.

Page 138: **film clips of Philip Zimbardo's 1971 Stanford Prison Experiment:** "Feature Film – The Stanford Prison Experiment (Documentary)," *YouTube,* accessed October 5, 2021, https://youtu.be/L_LKzEqlPto.

Page 138: **at Abu Ghraib during the Iraq War. We look at Specialist Charles Graner as he crouches above a corpse covered with contusions in a body bag.** "The Abu Ghraib Prison Photos." *AntiWar.com,* February 16, 2006. https://original.antiwar.com/news/2006/02/16/the-abu-ghraib-prison-photos/

I first saw renditions of the Abu Ghraib Prison photos in David Griffith's excellent essay collection, *A Good War is Hard to Find: The Art of Violence in America,* (Soft Skull Press, 2016), which were originally published on *AntiWar.com.*

Page 140: **"Stare. It is the only way to educate your eye, and more. Stare, pry, listen, eavesdrop. Die knowing something. You are not here long."**: Walker Evans qtd in Tom Barone and Elliot W. Eisner eds, 39 *Arts Based Research,* (SAGE Publications, 2012).

THE BELLY OF DESIRE

Page 149: "I was looking at myself in the mirror. I wish I had a pot. A pot belly....If I had one, I'd wear a T-shirt two sizes too small to accentuate it.": "Bruce Willis: Butch Coolidge, *Pulp Fiction* (1994)," *IMDB*, accessed October 7, 2021. https://www.imdb.com/title/tt0110912/characters/nm0000246.

SO MANY WAYS

Page 159: ...**if I tripped and dropped the baby, and he smashed into a brick retaining wall like in that short story by Lorrie Moore:** Lorrie Moore, "Terrific Mother," *Birds of America*, (Picador, 1999), 252, First published 1998.

In the story, "Terrific Mother," the baby's death is the inciting incident for the protagonist, Adrienne. Having been responsible for the accident that caused the baby's death, she must face crippling depression coupled with agoraphobia.

The accident happens at a Labor Day picnic. Adrienne is sitting on a picnic table, when the "dowels rotting in the joints, wobbled and began to topple her." Then in a flash of brilliance, Moore renders the tragic act in one sentence:

"And when she fell backward, wrenching her spine—in the slowed quickness of this flipping world, she saw the clayey clouds, some frozen faces, one lone star like the nose of a jet—and when the baby's head hit the stone retaining wall of the Spearsons' newly terraced yard and bled fatally into the brain, Adrienne went home shortly thereafter, after the hospital and the police reports, and did not leave her attic apartment for seven months, and there were fears, deep fears for her, on the part of Martin Porter, the man she had been dating, and on the part of almost everyone, including Sally Spearson, who phoned tearfully to say that she forgave her, that Adrienne might never come out."

I first read this story approximately sixteen years before I became a mother, and it was one of the haunting memories my brain dredged up during my postpartum anxiety.

Page 165: **In all the instances in which a child had been killed from being forgotten in the car, the same factors kept showing up: "stress, emotion, lack of sleep, and change in routine":** Gene Weingarten, "Forgetting a Child in the Backseat of a Car Is a Horrifying Mistake. Is It a Crime?" *Washington Post*, March 8 2009, https://www.washingtonpost.com/lifestyle/magazine/fatal-distraction-forgetting-a-child-in-thebackseat-of-a-car-is-a-horrifying-mistake-is-it-a-crime/2014/06/16/8ae0fe3a-f580-11e3-a3a5-42be35962a52_story.html.

Page 165: **According to local columnist Nick Jimenez, canicular days are mid-July to mid-August, signaling the most brutal heatwave of the year:** Nick Jimenez, "Dog Days of Summer Make Everyone Crazy, Including Government Officials," *Caller-Times*, August 5, 2017, https://www.caller.com/story/news/columnists/nick-jimenez/2017/08/05/dog-days-summer-make-everyone-crazy-including-government-officials/538841001/.

WHAT CANNOT BE HELPED

Page 176: **"with all the fierce rigidity of first motherhood...like all the books said":** Tillie Olsen, "As I Stand

Here Ironing (1961)," *Arguing About Literature*, 2nd ed. John Schilb and John Clifford, eds, (Bedford St. Martin's, 2017), 301-7.

Page 177: **One small study had concluded anesthesia exposure in children under the age of 2 were more like to have language and speech difficulties:** Salynn Boyles, "Anesthesia Before Age 2 Linked to Learning Problems," *WebMD*, October 3, 2011. https://www.webmd.com/children/news/20111003/anesthesia-before-age-2-linked-to-learning-problems.

Page 177: **A study of Danish birth cohorts…showed that by age sixteen there was no discernable cognitive or academic difference between children that had had anesthesia and those that hadn't:** Rachel Fields, "5 Recent Findings on Anesthesia in Children," *Becker's ASC Review*, June 1, 2011, https://www.beckersasc.com/anesthesia/5-recent-findings-on-anesthesia-in-children.html.

Page 177: **The cognitive risks of anesthesia in pediatric patients are unknown. We need more studies to fully understand the effects of anesthesia on developing brains, hearts, and lungs:** This is paraphrased from my memory. I remember being frustrated at the lack of certainty, which at the time struck me as poignant because the research findings I had read about the cognitive effects of anesthesia on children were a tangle of contradictory results.

Page: 183: **"To sift, to weigh…I will become engulfed":** Tillie Olsen, "As I Stand Here Ironing."

PANCAKES ARE JUST PANCAKES

Page 186: **During the hot summer months, our local morgues filled, so morticians used refrigerated semi-trucks from FEMA to hold dead bodies.** Sarah R. Champagne, "As Texas Morgues Fill Up, Refrigerator Trucks are on the Way in Several Counties," *The Texas Tribune*, July 10, 2020. https://www.texastribune.org/2020/07/10/texas-coronavirus-deaths-morgues-capacity/.

Page 187: "If you give a pig a pancake...she'll want some syrup to go with it": Laura Numeroff and Felicia Bond, *If You Give a Pig a Pancake*, (Harper Collins, 1998), First Published 1985.

Page 187: "What you do...if you have little kids, is lead as normal a life as possible, only with more pancakes": Marjorie Williams, "Hit by Lightning," *The Woman at the Washington Zoo: Writings on Politics, Family, and Fate*, (Public Affairs, 2006).

"Hit By Lightning" was published a year after Williams died at age forty-seven. It is the best essay I've read about facing a life-threatening illness, and it has echoed in my memory over a decade after I first read it.

Page 188: "What is it that smears the windows of the senses? Thought, convention, self-interest": Evelyn Underhill, *Practical Mysticism*, (Ariel Press, 1987), First Published 1914.

Page 188: "If the doors of perception were cleansed...everything would appear to man as it is—Infinite. But the doors of perception are hung with the cobwebs of thought, prejudice, cowardice, sloth": William Blake qtd in Evelyn Underhill, *Practical Mysticism*.

Page 190: "When you enter the water, something like a metamorphosis happens...you go through the looking-glass surface and enter a new world": Roger Deakin, *Waterlog: A Swimmer's Journey Through Britain,* (Tin House Books, 2021), First published 1999.

CANCER IS CLICHÉ

Page 195: "When you're ill you instinctively fear a diminishment and disfigurement of yourself": Anatole Broyard, *Intoxicated By My Illness: and Other Writings on Life and Death,* (Fawcett Columbine, 1992).

After his death, Broyard became controversial because it was revealed he'd spent his life passing as white, though he was Black. Identity politics aside, I've found his viewpoint of life-threatening illness invaluable, unique, and fresh.

Page 196: "a kind of bird with the governor turned low": Edward Hoagland, *The Courage of Turtles,* (North Point Press, 1985), First published 1968, 20.

This quote is the famous first line of the titular essay. "The Courage of Turtles" echoes the butterfly parable in *Zorba the Greek* as a poignant tale of a well-intentioned intervention going wrong. I highly recommend it.

Page 197: **The group boasted 5,300 members:** *Active & Fit with no Thyroid,* Private Facebook Group, accessed October 8, 2021, https://www.facebook.com/groups/947394471979074/.

At the time of writing, Active & Fit with no Thyroid, was still an active Facebook group with the mission to be "A stress free zone for those who are living with no thyroid or have a thyroid disease and wish to find inspiration and support through their journey in fitness and health. Our primary focus here is to help inspire, motivate. and support each other through activity, clean eating and encouraging others through experience strength and hope."

Page 200: "**The healthiest way of being ill is one most purified of, most resistant to, metaphoric thinking**": Susan Sontag, *Illness as Metaphor,* (Anchor/Doubleday, 1990). First published 1977.

Page 201: "**Metaphors may be as necessary to illness as they are to literature.... only metaphor[s] can express the bafflement, the panic combined with beatitude, of the threatened person**": Anatole Broyard, *Intoxicated By My Illness.*

Page 204: "**Stories have to repair the damage that illness has done to the ill person's sense of where she is in life.... Stories are a way of redrawing maps and finding new destinations**": Arthur W. Frank, *The Wounded Storyteller. (U of Chicago P,* 2013).

"**The romantic view is that illness exacerbates consciousness**": Susan Sontag. *Illness as Metaphor.*

Page 205: "**the calamity of disease can clear the way for insight into lifelong self-deceptions and failures of character**": Susan Sontag. *Illness as Metaphor.*

FROM BIRTH TO BONE

Page 208: **St. Luke's United Methodist Church offers online services at slumcorpuschristi.org**: The church's real website has an extra "c" for church in it, which I dropped to emphasize slum. The real address is https://slumccorpuschristi.org/, accessed October 19, 2001.

Page 210: **A group of perched vultures is called a wake:** "Turkey Vulture Tidbits," *Audubon California: Kern River Preserve*, 1998, accessed October 26, 2021, http://www.kern.audubon.org/tvfacts.htm

Page 211: **Texas Department of State Health Services reports that 210 people died of hypothermia:** Marc Marcella, "How Widespread and How Extreme was the Texas Freeze and Why?" *AIR 3*, June 2021, https://www.air-worldwide.com/blog/posts/2021/6/how-widespread-and-how-extreme-was-the-texas-freeze-and-why/

Page 213: "**Compassion is our capacity to relate in a tender and sympathetic way to what we perceive....embrace our pain with the kindness of a mother holding her child**": Richard Rohr, "Cultivating Compassion: Daily Meditations," *Center for Action and Contemplation*, October 1, 2021, https://cac.org/cultivating-compassion-2021-10-01/

Page 214: "**Heal the sick, soothe the suffering, comfort the afflicted, and shield the joyful**": "An Order for Compline: Daily Office," *The Book of (Online) Daily Prayer*, accessed on October 15, 2021, https://www.bcponline.org/

Page 183-4: "**Bones represent our truest and barest self...our home and anchor in the physical world**": Tommaso Fagiolo, "Bones in Customs and Arts: a Brief Anthropology, *Tommaso Fagioli: Words*, accessed October 15, 2021, http://tommasofagioli.com/ideas/anthropology-bones/

Page 185: **A quick Google search revealed that these turkey vultures were migrating:** "Turkey Vulture," *Hawk Watch International: Conserving Raptors and Our Shared Environment*, accessed October 12, 2021, https://hawkwatch.org/learn/factsheets/item/377-turkey-vulture.

BEFORE IT'S NIGHT ONCE MORE

Page 187: **My risk: 1 in 350**: "Frequency of Down Syndrome per Maternal Age." *Down Syndrome: Health Issues*, accessed October 15, 2021, http://www.ds-health.com/risk.htm

Page 188: **Of all cancer cases in the U.S., 3.8 percent of them are thyroid cancer:** Quang T. Nguyen, et al, "Diagnosis and Treatment of Patients with Thyroid Cancer," *American Health and Drug Benefits* 8, no. 1: (Feb 2015): 30, https://www.ncbi.nlm.nih.gov/pmc/articles/PMC4415174/

"**18 percent of the babies had serious birth defects, ranging from heart problems to cleft palate and extra fingers**": "Risk of Birth Defects in the Babies of Women with Thyroid Disease. *American Thyroid Association*, February 11, 2002, https://www.thyroid.org/risk-of-birth-defects-in-the-babies-of-women-with-thyroid-disease/

Page 190: "**Shoulder dystocia occurs in 0.2 to 3 percent of deliveries**": Henry Alexander Easley, III and Todd Michael Beste, "A Study of the Diagnostic Accuracy of an Existing Multivariable Test to Predict Shoulder Dystocia," *American Journal of Perinatology Reports* 9, no. 3 (July 2019), https://www.ncbi.nlm.nih.gov/pmc/articles/PMC6702026/

"**When a woman gives birth, death holds her hand for a little while**": Betty Smith, *A Tree Grows in Brooklyn*.

Page 190-1: "…approached death. You go down into places it's hard to get at in life, you know? ….I thought I was exploding. Like literally: becoming a star": Elisa Albert, *After Birth,* (Houghton Mifflin Harcourt, 2015).

This should be required reading for any woman considering pregnancy. I first read it while pregnant and Albert's thoughtful rendering of pregnancy took away a lot of the shame and stigma of childbirth and early motherhood without sugarcoating it.

Page 192: **Only about 10-15 percent of thyroid nodules like mine prove malignant:** Sophia C. Kamran, et al. "Thyroid Nodule Size and Prediction of Cancer." *The Journal of Clinical Endocrinology & Metabolism* 98, no 2, (1 Feb 2013): 564. https://academic.oup.com/jcem/article/98/2/564/2833083 15 Oct 2021.

Anesthesia-related mortality rates are 0.4 out of 100,000: Andre Gottschalk et al. "Is Anesthesia Dangerous?" *Dtsch Arztebl Int.*108, no. 27 (8 July 2011): 469. https://www.ncbi.nlm.nih.gov/pmc/articles/PMC3147285/

Page 195: **The 5-year survival rate is almost 100 percent for localized follicular cancers like mine:** "Thyroid Cancer Statistics. *Cancer.Net.* Feb 2021. https://www.cancer.net/cancer-types/thyroid-cancer/statistics

"That the future is unknowable is, for some, God's means of suturing us in, or to, the present moment:" Maggie Nelson. *Bluets.* (Wave Books, 2009).

Page 196: "**One day we were born, one day we shall die, the same day, the same second…** Birth astride of a grave, the light gleams an instant, then it's night once more." Samuel Beckett, *Waiting for Godot*. Act II. *Samuel-Beckett. Net,* accessed October 15, 2001, https://www.samuel-beckett.net/Waiting_for_Godot_Part2.html

ACKNOWLEDGEMENTS

I am grateful for the support this book received during all its stages.

Thank you to my editor, Jay Kristensen Jr. and the wonderful team at Unsolicited Press, including Summer Stewart and Alexis Gonzales.

Thank you to the literary journal editors who first published some of these essays, including Stephanie G'Schwind, Robert Stewart, Brett Lott, Jon Tribble, Lee Ann Roripaugh, Sheila Squillante, Lisa Duff, Nick Lantz, and Joshua Bohnsack. Thanks to Robert Atwan for choosing essays included here as notable in *Best American Essays*.

The following essays previously appeared (sometimes in different forms) in the following journals:

"From Birth to Bone," was first published in *Triquarterly* (Summer/Fall 2022), a publication of Northwestern University

"All from an Egg" (early version of "Holy Diminishment"), *The Texas Review* (Spring 2022).

"Making Headcheese," *Crab Orchard Review* (Winter 2019)

"The Belly of Desire," *Crazyhorse* (Spring 2016)

Reprinted in *Beautiful Flesh* (Colorado State Center for Literary Publishing, 2017).

"Killing Chickens," *New Letters* (Spring 2015)

New Letters Readers' Choice Nonfiction Award 2015

Notable Essay Best American Essays 2016

"Driving the Section Line," *The Fourth River* (Spring 2015)

Republished on *PenDust Radio Podcast* (Oct 2020)

"Dad's Kitchen Table" (early excerpt of "Driving the Section Line") *South Dakota Review*. (Summer 2013)

Notable Essay Best American Essays, 2015

"Lightning Flowers," *Colorado Review* (Fall 2013)

Notable Essay Best American Essays 2014

Republished on *PenDust Radio Podcast* (Aug 2022)

Thank you to my encouraging and rigorous professors at the Georgia College MFA program including Peter Selgin, Dr. Allen Gee, Laura Newbern, Dr. Bruce Gentry, and Dr. Martin Lammon.

Thank you to my friends and MFA cohort who workshopped some of these essays, including Monica Prince, Aimee Lewis Reau, Kate St. Ives, Amy Landau, Mary Kay McBrayer, Brandy Hawkins, Mac McCook Hulbert, Roger Sollenberger, Claire Helakowski, Chelsie Ruiz Rivera, Janet Dale, Rori Meyer, Sara Stephens Loomis, Georgia Knapp, Ruby Holsenbeck, Sandra Worsham and Shane Moritz.

Thank you to my writing critique groups for feedback and tough love, including Alyson Greene, Allyson Larkin, Maritza

Ramos, Monique Ruiz, Sandra Elle, David Carpenter, Bob James, Devorah Fox, Philly Vasquez, Kim Morrow, Cope Cumpston, Patrice McMahon, and Beth Barrett.

Thank you to the Writers' Studio of Corpus Christi instructors and support group members who've commiserated with and encouraged me, including Michael Quintana, Dr. Robin Carstensen, Michelle Stevenson, Omar Lopez, Jeff Moss, and Heather Stark.

Thank you to my friends Cynthia McKenna, James Dunham, Paul Michaels and Benjamin Volk.

Thank you to my family for being good sports about appearing in a memoir, including Rolland Krahulik, Carollee Bauhard Krahulik, Holly French, Erin Defruiter, Sam Heermans, and Karen Lenz Heermans.

Thank you to Stanley for being a surprising source of inspiration. Thank you, Kent, for your unwavering belief in my writing and your unfailing love.

About the Author

Sarah K. Lenz grew up in central Nebraska. Her creative nonfiction has appeared in *Colorado Review*, *New Letters*, *Triquarterly*, *TheFourth River*, *Pen Dust Radio* and elsewhere. Her work has been named Notable in *Best American Essays* three times. She writes the newsletter *Spirit: Notes for the Creative Contemplative*. Sarah is an Assistant Professor of English at Del Mar College in Corpus Christi, Texas where she lives with her husband, son, and twelve typewriters. Find her online at <u>sarahklenz.com</u>.

About Unsolicited Press

Unsolicited Press based out of Portland, Oregon and focuses on the works of the unsung and underrepresented. As a womxn-owned, all-volunteer small publisher that doesn't worry about profits as much as championing exceptional literature, we have the privilege of partnering with authors skirting the fringes of the lit world. We've worked with emerging and award-winning authors such as Shann Ray, Amy Shimshon-Santo, Brook Bhagat, Kris Amos, and John W. Bateman.

Learn more at unsolicitedpress.com. Find us on twitter and instagram.

CPSIA information can be obtained
at www.ICGtesting.com
Printed in the USA
BVHW041949160523
664275BV00003B/45